WELCOME TO THE ROOM, MAMA

The Mompreneur's Guide To Getting
Out Of Your Head, Ditching The Mom
Guilt, And Building A Successful Business

Alyssa Morton

Wishing you continued success!
-♡ alyssa morton

WELCOME TO THE ROOM, MAMA

THE MOM-PRENEUR'S GUIDE TO GETTING OUT OF
YOUR HEAD, DITCHING THE MOM GUILT, AND
BUILDING A SUCCESSFUL BUSINESS

ALYSSA MORTON

Cover Design by 100 Covers

For more information: lyss@lyssmorton.com

ISBN: 979-8-9876244-0-1

HERE'S A GIFT
BEFORE YOU EVEN BEGIN!

I appreciate you taking the time to purchase my book. As a thank you, here's a bonus gift to help you take action and have fun.

Some of the free resources in this book include:

- The Welcome To The Room, Mama Workbook
  - Identify Your Limiting Mindsets Worksheet To Debunk The Mindsets That Hold You Back
  - Create Your Vision Worksheet To Dominate Your Life
  - Create Solutions Worksheet To Get Out Of Your Head
  - Maximize Your Time Scheduling Planner To Maximize Your Productivity
  - The Perfect Morning Routine Planner To Fill Your Own Cup

- o Community Networking Guide To Build Your Room
- o Build Your Marketing Plan Worksheet To Strategize A Successful Marketing Plan
- o Niches Get Riches Worksheet To Identify Your Target Audience
- o Get In The Room Worksheet To Elevate Your Network
- o Create Your Client Experience Worksheet To Find Your Unique Process
- o Budget Planner Guide For Financial Success
- o Sales Mindset Success To Close More Deals
- o Leadership Journal For Self Development
- Printable Planners To Help You Maximize Your Productivity
- Budget Planner Spreadsheet Template To Create Financial Success
- The Resources That Will Help You Save Time As A Mompreneur

Get Your Free Gifts Here: Https://www.lyssmorton.com/book

Dedication

To my Lailah and Lisianne, thank you for giving me every reason possible to create the best version of myself, create the businesses and financial future I desire, and create a life filled with joy.

I hope to inspire you, set a positive example for you to go after your dreams, and to create a life that brings abundance, memories, and pure joy.

To my husband, thank you for providing the support financially, emotionally, and physically to encourage me to pursue my goals and dreams. Without you, this book, my businesses, and the vision for our future would not be possible.

Contents

I had enough

Twelve years of wasting away in a windowless office, my only "view" being the picturesque moutainscape on my computer screen, was more than long enough. The only sound louder than the office phone was the sound of someone taking a shit in the bathroom adjacent to my closet-sized office. It had my ear-holes ringing louder than a church bell on Sunday.

Did I mention the smell? You know the one?

A cleaning lady came in every couple of weeks, but my boss told her not to clean my "office." Instead, he left a plastic container of wipes on the filing cabinet for me. Since I never knew when I would see a replacement, I often had to soak up the leftover chemical solution in the container with paper towels.

Biohazard aside, the cherry on top of this cake was the complete dismissal of my last fifteen suggestions for running the office more like an actual doctor's office —not some casual hang out.

At the time, the prospect of a steady full-time job was enough to con me into the position. After years of struggling to function in an office that looked half-finished, and no opportunities for advancement or improvement presenting themselves, I began to realize my worth. The measly paychecks were insulting, but no amount of money would ever be enough of an incentive to sit in this *literal* shit hole. I mean –every Monday, I walked in to see mouse droppings covering my desk.

None of this helped my nausea. At nearly twelve weeks pregnant, I was still suffering from peak first-trimester symptoms. The doctors called it "morning sickness," but what they really meant was "all day sickness." During the first twenty weeks of my first pregnancy, I lost ten pounds because I couldn't eat –and if I did, nothing stayed down. My husband would come home from work and immediately shower. Otherwise, the scent of fumes, gas, and oil from his job would make me vomit. This second pregnancy wasn't as bad, but mouse droppings would make me sick on a non-pregnant day, anyway.

I had too many ideas and too much ambition for my worth to be valued at only a few hundred dollars a week. Not even an entire month's pay at this job would cover my mortgage, let alone the rest of my expenses with a baby on the way.

The turning point came when I finally asked myself, "What kind of mom would I be if I showed my baby girls that my ideas were invalid, that my life amounted only to submitting health insurance claims, and that it was fine to let my ambition die at that mouse dropping wasteland? What would it do to their own dreams and self-esteem if I continued to sit at the desk that brings absolutely no joy, fulfillment, or growth in return for so little money?"

Every week, I would revisit my goals with my husband and remember that this was a dead-end job. No health insurance, no paid time off, no retirement plan, no growth. The only perk that held me captive was the flexibility it gave me to create my own hours and spend more quality time with family. Looking back now, I'm ashamed at how many times we had that conversation without following through with action.

I shouldn't be too hard on myself, though. Previously, I had spoken with my boss at every annual review about my next phase of growth. I repeatedly asked for opportunities to advance in my position. Usually, he kept me hooked with a glimmer of hope. Sometimes, it was the prospect of leading the opening of another location. Other times, it was that I could create buzz for the business to bring in more patients.

"That first conversation happened at least five years ago," I told my husband, "and nothing has changed since then." If anything, the years of false hope and repeated dismissal had probably made me more complacent.

When it came to my final year at that job, I had already tried to quit three times. My attempts to quit usually arose from the frustration of feeling undervalued. As the office manager, I was the receiver and the filter for the staff's concerns. Even though I agreed with their frustrations, most complaints I passed along to the owner were ignored.

I finally started searching for other local jobs and went to some interviews. Before I knew it, I had a new job offer that made it feel less risky to quit. Of course, the threat of losing me resulted in a raise —one that was three years overdue. Tragically, I stayed because it was comfortable.

Comfort was my enemy. I was addicted to feeling safe. A comfortable job was one that I could always count on to be the same, where I knew what to expect, and I knew my limits. Comfort also meant that nothing changed if nothing changes. Ultimately, the change that needed to be made on my journey of personal growth was actually my career.

A dead-end job was not going to give me the challenges that I needed to overcome. It wasn't going to provide the fulfillment in overcoming those challenges. A dead-end job wouldn't prove to my daughters that they can achieve anything they want in this life. It wouldn't make me the example that I should be for them in any sense.

Instead, a dead-end job was simply a short-sighted source of income that would not support my growing family, goals, or ambitions. I needed to have those hard conversations with my husband and my boss, but this time, I needed to truly mean it.

Finally, I told him I was done, and that he had two weeks to find my replacement. In his typical way, he tried to prolong my presence there by asking if I could stay until he found and trained my replacement. Upon pushback, he desperately said that any hours I could work would be helpful, even if it was once every two weeks.

I hadn't fully learned my lesson until I agreed to this ridiculous request and wasted even more time in this new term of agreement. Nothing was actually going to change until I gave him a hard cut-off.

"I'm done at the end of this month. I created a manual for your replacement to use when training, so she can call me if she needs help."

Even then, I had given too much of my valuable time and talents to this business owner. It never should have been my job to write up that manual or to volunteer even more time helping the replacement after I had quit. But I realized that if I didn't give the hard deadline and actually follow through, that four-square-foot office would become my coffin. I was going to be working in that migraine-inducing environment of flickering fluorescent lights, rodents, and that god-forsaken smell emanating from the bathroom.

Not my monkey, not my circus, right?

Each time my suggestion was rejected, each time a staff complaint was ignored, I thought about how my business would be different.

I dreamed about my business for three years, even when I felt that I had no right to start my own business. Even when my dream job was something I had never come close to doing before. I dreamed of flower fields full of dahlias. I dreamed of the ability to sell flowers to earn a living. That had to be enjoyable, right? The creativity. The passion. The ambition. The respect. My ideas would be valued for what they're truly worth.

It would be *my business.*

Having my own business meant that I could set the foundation for the way staff and clients should be treated. I would finally be able to take charge of my life, work or not work when I wanted. I could customize my life and business to compliment each other as perfectly as I desired. Income earning was exponential and limitless. I could taste the financial freedom.

Over the course of one year, my husband and I worked our asses off to pay our debts. We had been working our jobs consistently full-time, even overtime when we could, and took any opportunity that presented itself for a quick buck to get that much closer to zero. For the first time in our lives, we locked in on a budget and stuck to it.

Like many young couples, we had spent too many days going out to restaurants or getting takeout for breakfast, lunch, and dinner. When the day was done, we wondered how twenty-five thousand dollars of credit card debt accumulated so quickly.

Twenty-five thousand dollars of credit card debt felt like we had been buried alive. The thought of bringing a baby into the world *again* with the lack of financial security felt like a crime against my children. At the time, it seemed irresponsible to quit my job, even when I had hated it since my first day.

As my mindset changed, I realized that my business could be created to pay off our debts, fuel our financial freedom, and bring joy to our family. It had the power to change *everything*.

My business plan had been sitting in my Google Drive folder for nearly a year as I worked up the courage to start with another baby on the way. I had it all figured out: I planned to launch my flower business in time for Valentine's Day. I planned to spread word to the community early in the year so that, come wedding season, they would know I was there and available.

Solid marketing strategy? Eh, it barely qualified. But I knew that if I started immediately, I could make it better over time. I knew I would have room to improve once I had some momentum, practice, and photos to market my business.

I said, "Just start, Lyss."

- -

Becoming a mom-preneur has its struggles –I know that intimately. From time management struggles to mom guilt, lack of support, and limiting mindsets, we have an uphill battle to create the destiny we desire. As you're reading my story, I'm positive that you're at least finding bits and pieces that strike you right to the core. You've experienced them firsthand. Who hasn't had to take that terrible first job in exchange for experience or a paycheck to survive on? Who hasn't been told, "Just get your foot in the door for now, it'll get better later?"

Time and time again, that paycheck stays the same. Time and time again, women *just* survive. Time and time again, it doesn't get better.

Breaking that cycle will be the most profound thing you can do as a woman, as a mom, and as a passionate soul with big ideas. Becoming a mom-preneur will be the most fulfilling journey as you act on your calling to become the truest version of yourself.

Throughout the course of this book, I am going to walk you through my four-phase process of becoming a mom-preneur. I'll cover topics like overcoming mindset barriers, resolving time management struggles, implementing your business idea, and finally bringing to life the future you've envisioned for your family. Within each phase, we will tackle every limiting mindset that I have experienced during my journey of entrepreneurship while raising two kids under two years old. I have personally seen each of these mindsets keep mom-preneurs from beginning their journey for success and from continuing the journey when it gets tough.

Along with each mindset, you'll read about my firsthand experiences with the beliefs that could have kept me from my dreams. You'll also read how that business has evolved to become five other businesses with no end of ambition in sight. I have even bigger goals and the drive to make it all happen for me, my kids, and my future.

Ultimately, you'll be able to apply these lessons learned. You can avoid the huge mistakes I've made, or at least you can solve them if you're currently in the same boat that I was. As you read this book, I encourage you to follow along in the workbook, too. I've linked resources so that you are able to overcome your limiting beliefs, identify potential time distractions, and create an action plan that suits your business growth and needs. With this detailed plan and reframed mindset, you'll be able to implement the process of becoming a mom-preneur so that you can fulfill the purpose you've chosen for your life.

Phase 1: Curating the Mom-Preneur Mindset

Limiting beliefs hold you back from beginning something new, both as a mom and a professional. Change is scary, so the first thing the mind does is spiral into catastrophic thinking. In other words, you'll begin creating and replaying the worst possible scenarios in your head so that you can justify your avoidance of change. Typical mindsets that stop moms from even starting something new are:

"I am a mom, so it's selfish for me to do anything I enjoy without my kids involved."

"I am a mom, and that's a full-time job. I can't start a business."

"My kids need me around the clock, so I don't have time to dedicate to anything extra."

"When my kids graduate from school —that's when I'll be able to start my life."

"Everyone will see me as selfish for following my passions."

Do any of these phrases sound familiar to the voice in your head right now?

The mind is a powerful tool. You can use your mind to fixate on the problems in your life and draw up excuses. Or, you can use your mind to create innovative solutions so that you can have your cake and eat it, too.

As a mom, you are resilient, you are strong, you are motivated, and you have the power to create the future that you want for yourself and your children. If anyone can do it, you *certainly* can.

It's not selfish to want to create a business that fuels your creativity, inspires you to do better in the world, or empowers your children to follow their passions. In fact, when mothers feel fulfilled in their life, the joy and fulfillment pours out of them and improves the lives of their children and everyone around them.

I've never been so fulfilled in my life then I have been as an entrepreneur. When I gave birth to my first daughter, still working in that shithole, I felt disconnected and unhappy. I wasn't able to experience my life and the birth of my daughter as I should have because I wasn't centered within myself. The role I worked in was not yet the one I deserved.

After I had my second daughter and was deep in the throes of entrepreneurship, I was working more than I ever had before. Even in that level of uncertainty, instability, and serious struggle, I felt fulfilled in my soul, more connected to my kids, and more confident in myself accomplishing my goals.

You have the power to create the life envisioned for yourself and your kids, not anyone else. Your boss isn't forcing you to keep your terrible dead-end job –you're just giving them the power to manipulate and use you. You need to shift your mindset to believe that you can learn and improve each day, overcome imposter syndrome, and begin your experience somewhere. You are more than capable of overcoming your fears of failure or success (yes, that's a thing!). You have everything you need to beat your perfectionism personality traits, and you can create a community of support that will help you accomplish goals you never thought were possible.

The mom-preneur journey begins with having the right mindset. Lack, scarcity, and limiting mindsets have a way of easily creeping into our lives. Each step of the way —as you think about beginning your journey, starting the process, and implementing your action plan —the voice inside your head can either constantly kick you down, or it can build you up. Every moment you live the mom-preneur life, it's within your power to self-deprecate or to forge forward, proud and confident.

For you to fast-track your mom-preneur path to success, it's important that we identify common limiting mindsets, understand how they can affect you, and implement strategies to shift these mindsets so you feel empowered in your mom-preneur lifestyle.

Throughout the course of my development as a mom-preneur, I've encountered all of the limiting beliefs that you'll read about here. Each mindset has impacted my ability to get out of my own way, but each person is unique in which limiting beliefs are the most challenging to them. I'll share my stories with you so that you realize you aren't alone. Instead of feeling isolated, crazy, or afraid, you can feel empowered to overcome your own limiting beliefs to start your journey. I urge you to continue to make the choice daily to be the best version of yourself as a mom and entrepreneur.

In this first chapter, we are going to break down all of the limiting beliefs I've encountered in the first phase of developing my business —overcoming "just being a mom" or an "inexperienced wannabe." While reading my experiences, please follow along in the workbook to uncover your limiting mindsets. That way, we can reframe your limiting mindsets before diving into phase two of our mom-preneur journey together.

Limiting Mindset #1: "I don't know what to do."

My website was live. I spent about two hours crafting the social media post that would go out on Facebook to my list of family, friends, and frenemies. Praying that they wouldn't judge me. Praying that it wasn't too late to order their Valentine's Day flowers. Praying that it would work.

My armpits were sweating pools of liquid into my sweatshirt despite the office thermometer's setting of sixty degrees. My fingers froze as I typed out my message to ask for support. I sat in that tiny office, my chest tight with anxiety and my stomach fluttering. My blood pressure was rising to a dangerous degree. My small heater blew on my legs as I forced out a meaningful and enthusiastic message about my new adventure.

> You guys have all followed along as I met the love of my life, got married, had a sweet little girl, and now my sweet hubby and I have started a business!
>
> You know how much I love flowers. SO, we're going to grow our own specialty blooms, design them, and sell them within the community to florists, designers, and other flower lovers!
>
> Please follow along on my business page and check out our website.
>
> And check out our Valentine's Day sale! Save 10% on your order with code Vday21.
>
> Help us spread joy through flowers! Thanks flower friends.

I received many congratulations and "Good luck on this adventure!" comments. I also received a handful of orders from many of my acquaintances in support of my new journey. Ironically, most of the close friends that I thought supported me never sent in an order. Later, I saw their grocery store bouquets placed proudly on their Instagram stories.

Yikes.

I had created a rough recipe for fulfilling those orders, but quickly realized that there weren't enough flowers to accommodate the orders I received. I also didn't charge enough for the quality these customers were expecting.

I delivered anyway, choking down the experience as a lesson learned. I would price correctly next time.

That's business, I thought. *They'll love it and keep ordering.*

When I created my marketing plan, I wasn't sure exactly what I wanted to do. I just knew that flowers would be the medium. I had an inkling that I wanted to get involved with wedding and event design, but I also knew that I needed to earn money quickly.

In an effort to keep costs low while still getting the ball rolling, my husband and I broke our own backs starting up the business. We planted thousands of seeds in our garden, including hundreds of tulip bulbs and daffodil bulbs, and figured we could sell these home-grown flowers to our community.

We had read about the horrors of the floral industry and decided we could be a positive influence instead of contributing. Much of the industry imports its flowers from overseas and uses unsustainable mechanics and resources. Our refusal to contribute to this dark aspect of the floral industry –and instead educating our clients about it –would also be a great way to position ourselves in the market.

In my excitement to get my business started, and carried away by my passion for high-value, sustainable floral design, it hadn't crossed my mind who made up the local market.

I lived in a community that typically only valued flowers for special occasions, and grocery store floral departments were the most trafficked floral suppliers for the general population. Bouquets and corsages for special occasions were more of a quick pick-up on the way to events rather than carefully thought-through gifts. My community was full of customers who picked up flowers thinking, *Here's a twelve dollar bouquet of flowers for birthing me. Thanks, mom.*

That being said, my vision for the business did not align at all with the locals in my area. While they were happy gifting grocery store flowers, I was envisioning five-hundred-dollar custom arrangements that would adorn entry tables without wilting in just a few hours.

Three months after our seed-sowing, we prepared for Mother's Day weekend. In an effort to market my business and bring in revenue, I connected with a local elementary school to host a Mother's Day fundraiser.

I fully expected pricing to be an issue –as I was inexperienced with pricing and with florals –so I attempted to get ahead and explain my reasoning. I shared my recipe with them so they'd know what to expect and understand the pricing that came with it. *I had planted hundreds of tulips to bloom around that time*, I thought, *and since they're blooms from my garden, I could price a bit lower.*

Of course, nothing goes as planned. When Mother's Day was still three weeks away, my tulips all decided to pop open. There was no way they would still be useful for Mother's Day, so I quickly began problem-solving. In my research, I read that tulips could hold for weeks in a cooler space, so I sprung to get them inside our "cooler." Funny thing, though —my cooler was my downstairs bathroom. It wasn't properly insulated, so it hung around fifty degrees despite our best efforts; not the near-freezing temperatures needed to preserve the blooms for weeks.

Ouch. Another hard lesson learned. Again, I didn't charge enough to begin with, and now I couldn't even use the homegrown tulips as I had planned.

Even though I knew it wouldn't work, I still tried to use the tulips from our "cooler." Ouch ouch. Decaying tulips were not going to create beautiful bouquets cherished by the community on Mother's Day.

Once I admitted defeat, I panic-sourced additional blooms to make up for the bouquet orders we couldn't fulfill with our own flowers. We took a loss.

As the season went on, I thought the farmer's market would be a great place to sell my flowers. I eagerly approached my wholesaler, purchased hundreds of dollars of flowers, arranged some beautiful bouquets, and then I sat with them for six hours. It was hot, the flowers wilted, and nothing sold. I didn't get a pretty penny to make up for the hundreds I spent on my flowers, not to mention my time spent putting together the arrangements and sitting there all day.

At least my daughter came with me the first week and scored me a few sales. Who can resist an adorable nine-month-old little girl? Despite having a mascot, I quickly realized that this wasn't going to work for my needs, and I needed to make a change.

Another idea hits me —offer a weekly subscription for floral arrangement deliveries. That way, the community could enjoy our precious home-grown blooms without even leaving their homes.

Only one taker. I have so much love and appreciation for this man that supported our business, but his order wasn't enough to keep us afloat. It didn't help that my garden flowers didn't bloom in time for his order to be delivered, so I ended up needing to source more flowers again.

I didn't think that one all the way through, either.

Again and again, I tried to think of new ways to get my flowers into the community and create a good business for myself. Prom and graduation were coming soon, and I knew that could be a big opportunity for my business. A few seniors had contacted me to create prom bouquets to match their dresses. Of course, they all wanted different colored blooms, and they were the mean girls in school, if you know what I mean.

I was desperate to keep getting business, but it ended up costing me money. Different-colored bunches and sixty-dollar bouquets do not add up to a successful small business. To kick me while I was down, more than half of the girls' parents harassed me about their flowers wilting and wanting refunds.

Impossible, I thought. I knew how to process flowers, they just wanted to scam me out of my business. At the time, though, I had no real process in place for dealing with such complaints.

In a last ditch effort, I contacted the school superintendent to discuss selling flowers at graduation. These bouquets would be for all of the parents that didn't think to buy flowers before the ceremony began. We structured it as a fundraiser for the upcoming senior class so that it would benefit us both.

Some people gawked at my twenty-dollar bouquets –but hey, a pregnant girl has got to eat, and you didn't plan in advance!

I tried it all. That's the beauty of just starting, though: I learned everything that I didn't want to do ever again.

Here's another thing.

By trying out different aspects and market segments of the industry, practicing my trade, and putting myself out into the community, I learned a lot about the people with whom I didn't enjoy working. I found out which market segments I would avoid, and I realized which price points would never work for my vision.

I also realized that, based on my circumstances, designing out of my home studio with a fifty-degree bathroom cooler wasn't a sustainable situation. I needed to rethink my strategy.

Without a properly insulated cooler and a dedicated retail storefront, a retail-style business was never going to work successfully. I thought about the logistics, like how people want their flowers to last weeks when they order retail, and finally understood that it would be impossible for me to deliver on those expectations without the equipment and space.

Further, I realized I didn't want random customers coming to my house regularly, and the zoning department would be up my butt if they did.

In all this trial and error, I was wasting money and time. My current strategy was a recipe for bankruptcy.

All along, I was problem-solving the wrong thing. It wasn't that I needed to try to chameleon myself into whichever opportunity presented itself to make a quick buck. Instead, I should have been going after a market that fit my vision. The local population who adored grocery store bouquets for holidays was not my market, and that's completely fine. Other florists were a great fit for them. Instead, my home-design situation and vision for high-value floral design would best suit wedding and event services.

Hold on, do I hear a full circle coming? Yes… it just so happened that I had previously wanted to enter this space, as I really enjoyed this area of the industry.

Sounds like a win to me.

- -

"I don't know what to do" should actually be an exciting statement to experiment with in your business. Trial and error is truly the only way to learn if you like what you're doing. Just as we teach our kids to try new foods and activities, we need to follow the lesson of simply trying something new, even if it's uncomfortable.

By believing that your lack of knowledge is enough to stop you from trying, you're simply not moving the needle on anything. You'll never experience anything beyond what you've already experienced, so you'll never be anywhere doing anything other than what you're doing right now.

Are you comfortable where you are stuck?

If the answer is yes, then mom-preneurship isn't for you. If you aren't comfortable, then allowing yourself to be too scared to try will not improve the situation in which you're living. This less-than-satisfactory financial situation that you're experiencing, this lack of joy in your current job, is all here to stay unless you embrace doing something you know nothing about.

If you've been having this limiting belief circling in your head, keeping you from starting, then I urge you to pull out your workbook. I've linked it in the resource section so you can start hashing out what you're scared of and how you can face it.

Reframe your mindset to believe that there's nothing wrong with not knowing what to do. What's wrong is letting that get in the way of figuring out what to do. Remember, trying things out for the first time is a great way to learn what you never want to do again, just as much as it's a great way to find what you love. This forward stride of trial and error towards knowledge will help build momentum in your journey of self-development and entrepreneurship.

Limiting Mindset #2: "I have no experience."

I am not a floral designer. I have absolutely no business trying to convince couples to hire me for the most special day of their life, I thought.

These couples were investing thousands upon thousands of dollars into their momentous celebrations. I couldn't expect them to delegate even a fraction of that investment to me. Why would I believe I was worth that kind of money or consideration when I didn't even have a single event under my belt? When I hadn't ever put my skills to the test to bring such an important vision to life?

Typical me, a problem solver, scrambled my brain for solutions. How could I get the skills and experience I needed if I could never even begin? Then, it hit me. I realized that I could work for someone else as a freelancer.

In the floral industry, freelance designers are highly sought after. In the peak of post-pandemic wedding season, florists had become even more desperate for extra hands as they took on more bookings than they could ever really handle. Many of the designers in my area were completely overbooked and understaffed, opening opportunities for new designers to come into the field with basic skillsets. *Kismet,* I thought. I could practice my skills, build experience, learn from the best, and even start my portfolio, all while bringing other florists' visions to life.

All of the freelance opportunities I jumped on helped me become a better overall business owner. I didn't just improve my floral design skills –I started learning how to communicate with couples so that, when my business began to receive leads, I could communicate value, handle hiccups, and be confident in my own vision.

Suddenly, I had some photos, experience, and practice under my belt. Leads started coming my way from the fully-booked florists that declined their inquiries. Freelance turned into full-time business organically.

Talk about a beautiful opportunity.

- -

Mindset is the key to success when starting a new business.

The way that you think about yourself, goals, clients, money, and everything else impacts the decisions that you make when building and operating your business.

By allowing limiting beliefs to rule over you, like lacking the skillset to even begin your trade, you stop yourself from ever moving forward. No one is born with all the knowledge available to be a successful business owner in your field. Not even successful business owners in your field know everything there is to know –that's impossible! You're setting yourself up to fail, as you are limiting your ability to attract, sell, and satisfy your clients before you even pick up that phone or write that email.

Of course, the only way to gain and improve your skillsets is by practicing. In the business world, practice happens out in the field – only so much knowledge can be gained in a course or through research. Sometimes, you just have to endure the trial by fire. If it's applicable –and most of the time, it is –the first action you should take is to begin working in the field as an independent contractor for other professionals in your industry.

By learning the tricks of the trade firsthand, your knowledge and skills will grow faster than ever. You'll see how other business owners operate daily, which tools they favor, how they handle clients, and find shortcuts that would have taken you years to figure out on your own. Your speed, style, and abilities will grow incredibly under the pressure.

Turn your problems into solutions. Reframe the limiting mindset "I don't have experience" into "I have an opportunity to learn from the best early on so that I can run my business like someone who has years of experience." Turn the fear "I'll never be able to start because I don't have the skills" into an opportunity to fast track your career right out of the gate.

After all, this is a great problem to have. It means you haven't sunk your whole life building a business slowly because you struggled to prove your skills and gain experience. Creating momentum, and doing it quickly, is important as you work toward creating a life that you want for yourself. Learning is part of the journey, and you'll never stop learning. There is no destination, so *just start doing*.

Limiting Mindset #3: "Who am I to charge for this?"

Feelings of imposter syndrome quickly crept into my life as I began receiving inquiries for weddings and events. *I had only been in the industry for six months*, I thought, *who was I to fulfill someone's most special day in their life?*

"Fake it 'til you make it" was a common phrase in the entrepreneurial world, but it only solidified my feelings that I was a fraud. I had been freelancing for other florists, building my skills and experience, but I hadn't yet taken on an entire event on my own. My company couldn't *rightfully* claim that it had fulfilled a wedding order.

Pretend to be something I'm not? How would that create a successful business? I thought, *people will see right through me.*

I am a new mom.

I am only twenty-five years old.

I am a woman.

I have only been a florist for six months.

I'd be dismissed as soon as I got on that first call.

All of these thoughts crept into my mind, making me feel like I was not worthy of pursuing this career passion of mine. I thought, *no one will spend money on their wedding flowers to work with me, so why even try?*

One day, my mentor realized that my limiting mindsets were holding me back from using the talent I had spent half a year offering to other florists. She shined a light on my feelings of imposter syndrome and reminded me that time was an illusion in entrepreneurship. I did not need to be in the industry for ten years or even serve hundreds of events. As long as I had the necessary skill sets or could hire the people with the necessary skill sets, then I would be able to fulfill my contracts. That service was all clients really needed, and that was enough to charge the amount I deserved to be paid.

This realization blew my limiting beliefs out of the water –she was right. By believing that I was not worthy of charging a specific value, I would always be undercutting others in my industry, and my lack of self-esteem would also shine through my work. I would be self-deprecating, unsure of myself, and therefore seemingly unreliable and unworthy when communicating in my sales conversations.

She encouraged me to envision myself as a successful event florist. To attract the right clients and fulfill their orders using my full potential, I needed to *believe* I was an experienced and worthy event florist. I needed to be the event florist with a minimum spend requirement, that acted, dressed, and spoke like the version of the event florist I dreamed of becoming.

She reminded me that if I didn't see the value of my work, then my prospects wouldn't see the value in my work either.

Further, she reminded me that, even though I was only a business owner for six months, I could still accomplish my six-figure goal by year-end.

- -

Imposter syndrome shows up in your life when you are making positive changes. It makes you feel like someone else, like a fraud, just when you are working to become the best version of yourself. You think, *who am I to be trying to do this, speak like this, have this much confidence, and sell this service that I've never even provided before?*

Take comfort in this: imposter syndrome appears when you break free from your comfort zone. It appears when you make a good change in your life. It appears when you are stepping into your new power and a new version of yourself. It doesn't mean you are becoming a fraud –it actually means you're on the way to becoming exactly who you should be.

When you lean into your feelings of imposter syndrome, when you hide behind the excuses that arise from it, it impacts the way that you communicate in sales conversations. By believing you are a fraud, you come across as a fraud when talking to clients and making decisions in your business.

By overcoming these feelings of imposter syndrome and shifting your mindset to "act as if," you begin to speak like the professional you truly are.

What does it mean to "act as if?"

1. Envision the person that you want to be. How would they act? What would they wear? What would they say? Where do they shop? What do they eat? What does their office look like? How do they decorate their home, even?

2. Make a conscious decision to act like the person you want to become. Jump into this transformation with gusto, because you'll never actually become this person if you don't begin your transformation. When you decide to act like the person you want to be, you will slowly see yourself become this person.

The point I'm trying to make is that there's a difference between "faking it until you make it" and "acting as if." The first phrase has a deceitful undertone. It feels like you are purposefully manipulating other people into believing you are someone that you aren't. It has a yucky connotation that you're performing a disservice to yourself and the client. The second phrase, "acting as if," encourages you to become who you truly are inside. You use your mind to picture the best version of yourself so that you can begin behaving as the best version of yourself right now. It helps you take the actions required to become this positive version of yourself and level up in your career.

As you continue your entrepreneurial journey, you'll find imposter syndrome creeping into your life over and over again. It always appears as you begin to level up into a new version of yourself, pivot in a new direction, or start a new adventure. Change encourages you to step out of your comfort zone, making you feel like an imposter. But you aren't an imposter just because you're trying something new –remember that.

Before you know it, you'll be speaking, standing, walking, dressing, and acting like that new and improved version of yourself. Because you just *will be*.

Limiting Mindset #4: "I'm never going to succeed."

I have to be number one, I would think in kindergarten as the class lined up to walk the halls. My mom used to joke that I had "number one syndrome" because I needed to be at the top of the attendance roster, line leader, and the winner of every competition. It was an obsession.

In my recent discovery during self-development, I learned that I am an "enneagram three" to the core, so achievements are how I seek attention and feel loved.

As an enneagram three, also known as "the achiever," I have this deep-rooted personality trait that gives me the inner drive to succeed. Though, the side effect of this drive for success is the never-ending feeling that I am failing, and that I'll never be good enough to succeed.

My inherent fear of failure creates limiting beliefs deep in my core. It tells me that those around me will not love me if I fail, that I will embarrass myself and never recover, and that my value depends on my accomplishments and successes.

Since all of my greatest fears revolved around being unloved, unworthy, and embarrassed, failing would be catastrophic.

I've realized that my fear of failure and being unloved has a lot more to do with me than it does with anyone else. Because of this truth, we can safely label this fear as a limiting mindset. Once I discovered that most people were not even paying attention to anything I was doing, let alone criticizing every small detail of my actions, I felt a huge relief. Most people are too worried about their own accomplishments, fears, and lack of self-worth to see beyond themselves.

My fear of failure became much smaller —to fail was not that catastrophic if it didn't truly make anyone love me less. Now, I could reframe "failures" into "lessons learned" and use them as opportunities for feedback and improvement.

- -

Failure can be intimidating. It can be embarrassing. It can keep you from putting one foot in front of another. Understanding the root cause of your fear of failure can help to propel you forward by removing that limiting belief. Then, you can replace it with an empowering belief such as "failure is feedback for the future."

If you're anything like me, I've already done the work for you. By understanding that most people aren't looking at you the way that you think they are, you can remove that perceived spotlight on your failures. People live in their own world and selfishly think about their own problems. Their selfishness is a gift to you —they're not paying too much attention, if any, to your failures.

If you aren't like me, then you'll need to do some more digging on your own. From where do you think your fear of failure derives? When did it come about, and what makes it feel worse? What is the worst-case scenario for you when you fail?

Regardless of your unique root cause of fear, you can reframe that fear all the same. Look at your failures as feedback. Remove the emotion from the shortcoming and validate the future improvements that need to be made.

Limiting Mindset #5: "I'll never be good enough."

We just talked about my fear of failure, so I realize I might be backing up a bit, but there is another important aspect of my "achiever" personality trait. It is related to failure, but it deserves its own discussion. While my "achiever" personality caused me to be terrified of failure, it also created huge pauses in my life where I was reworking and reworking things to perfection.

This achiever personality trait of mine required me to consistently accomplish my goals, but they also needed to be completed perfectly. I needed everyone to enjoy the work that I had done to the maximum potential, which meant it needed to be perfect... or so I used to think.

Many times, I felt like I couldn't even get the ball rolling because I had the compulsive need to perfect something before the world would see it. I would waste so much time redoing things, analyzing every little detail, and thinking out every possible scenario and path. I might have somehow survived academically and in my younger years this way, but it was no way to begin my entrepreneurial journey.

Why? You can't have a business if you never even begin. There is no business to be had if it's impossible to perfect, so you just never start doing business. I can make you one promise: starting a new business is not something you can perfect.

So there I was, with my fear of failure and my perfectionism battling it out. I constantly needed to achieve, yet I couldn't because perfection is impossible. It wasn't until the achiever in me learned that I simply had to begin and follow through to achieve anything, even if the final product wasn't perfect, that I began making strides. Achieving a goal was something that required you to learn along the way, to take detours, and to get feedback when you made mistakes. As I set about achieving my goals, I could continually improve and go back to make the final product better.

After all this time as an entrepreneur, I've realized that insisting on perfection is actually to fail before you begin. Until I had tried something at least once, I could never even know what "perfect" looked like.

- -

Feeling that everything needs to be perfect before you begin simply prolongs your desired result. Perfection is impossible, and you're going to continually change your mind about what perfection looks like, too. Your goals become moving targets that were already too far out of your reach.

Perfectionism and the fear of failure are close cousins. As a recovering perfectionist, I learned the hard way that trying to get it perfect simply prolongs my struggle and keeps me stuck in place. I can never get the momentum I need for success. Consistently trying to create the perfect product, service, launch, or process is actually something we should laugh about. It's not just impossible –it's ironic!

The biggest lesson in entrepreneurship is that the feedback you receive from your clients is golden. They'll help you to fine-tune everything about your business simply by having opinions and sharing their experience with you honestly.

Guess what they can't do if you never give them any business to test out?

As long as you go into the business with a service-focused value, your clients will keep coming back even after mistakes. It's not the perfection of your products and services that counts, it's how you respond to those mistakes –both as a part of self-growth and as a part of improving your business. Great customer service is one of the leading reasons why clients refer businesses to their friends and family and keep patronizing your business, not perfection.

Giving yourself the grace to "do it messy" allows you to revisit each project and make it better over time. Business ownership is a work in progress. There's no such thing as perfection in an ever-evolving economy, market, and ideal clientele.

Even you are ever-changing, so embrace it. Your ideas will evolve, your brand will evolve, and your wisdom about your trade will evolve. Give yourself the grace to come back later and make it better so that you can roll with the momentum and see your growth over time.

Limiting Mindset #6: "I am not as successful as them."

Every step of the way, I struggle to remind myself that this is still my career's first chapter. I haven't had as many leads or bookings as most local florists. Their portfolios reflect large events, hundreds of raving couples, and referrals that overflow their calendar with meetings. I imagine their inbox bursting with confirmations and their bank accounts brimming with constant income.

I'm worth so much more than my self-deprecation. In my first year as an event florist, I should be proud of the events that I've booked and fulfilled. I should be grinning with joy over all of the five-star reviews I've received and for the clients that have turned into raving fans, spreading word-of-mouth everywhere. Instead of snooping around into every other florist's gorgeous client showcases, I need to compare myself to myself. I need to sit the *current me* down next to the *past me* because we need to have a chat.

I need to reflect on where I started and truly compare apples to apples rather than oranges. At the beginning of my floral journey, it did not look like this. In a decade, my business will likely be far larger and more successful than that of my industry peers that have already been in business for a decade or longer.

Do you see that? I shifted my mindset. Like magic, instead of thinking about how much further along I should be in my eighteen-month journey, comparing my extremely young business to decades-old businesses, I'm thinking about how quickly I've grown my business in only eighteen months.

In only eighteen months, I have:

- Booked nearly fifty clients for weddings and events
- Grossed six figures in revenue
- Obtained nearly fifty five-star reviews across all major platforms
- Created relationships and became a preferred vendor with many venues, photographers, cosmetic artists, planners, and more
- Launched a beautiful brand & website
- Re-structured my business operations for rapid growth
- Learned how to preserve event florals and package them as a product
- Fulfilled my first "luxury" wedding, and got a five-star review for it
- Used my sales prowess to turn a three-thousand dollar budget into a luxury wedding worth ten-thousand dollars in decor
- Learned to diversify my business to create multiple income streams
- Achieved a decent social media presence
- Started a YouTube Channel
- Joined a mastermind group and began creating one of my own
- Hosted my first ever Behind the Business Summit, complete with tons of interviews with other innovative and powerful business women
- Invested in myself

When I look back on the struggles that I've overcome as a postpartum mom of two under two, building my own business and brand, I remind myself that I really am doing well for my second year of business.

I have built my business with NO business debt. This business was literally generated from an idea in a closet-sized shithole. My skills have grown tremendously. Finally, my business is destined for greatness and success. It is just as good, if not better, than any other business in my industry that has been operating for decades. That satisfies my perfectionist-in-recovery self more than anything.

- -

Moms have a special capacity to handle hard things. We assume all responsibility for the house, the kids, and the fun memories we get to make with them. We take charge of setting them up to pursue their education, their dreams, and their destiny. While we struggle to keep our mental health in check, we worry more about how our spouses and children are getting through their day.

Everyone and everything comes before us –we put others before us so much that we forget something super important: As moms, our family needs us to be the best version of ourselves, but we can't do that if we don't take care of ourselves. We can't follow through on our commitments to them if we're barely surviving. We can't become who we're destined to be if we're too focused on everyone else.

It's vitally important for us moms to step back and honestly evaluate our growth. Being honest about our growth means realizing when we're being unfair to ourselves. Are we always working ourselves to the bone, always putting everyone else first to the point that we don't take care of ourselves? Do we give ourselves grace throughout the day, and forgive ourselves for our shortcomings and mistakes? Do we compare ourselves to *ourselves*, and not unfairly with other people in different circumstances?

Personal and professional life go hand-in-hand. The way we treat ourselves at home is likely the same way we treat ourselves in the office. When comparing your business to the success of other businesses, especially without fully seeing all of their details, we're being purposefully dishonest and hateful towards ourselves. Take out your journal to document all of your accomplishments since you started your journey. Document the big things and the small things and look back on your *own* growth.

Compare yourself to where you started and you will begin to realize just how special and important you are. Seeing just how much you juggle every day and still manage to accomplish major goals will fill you with more confidence to keep growing, developing, and creating success in your life and business.

Grab hold of the power to shift your mindset. Compare your growth to your own growth instead of someone else's growth. Empower yourself by focusing on yourself. Journal daily to track and review personal and professional growth, celebrate obstacles you've overcome, and keep your vision at the forefront of your mind to keep you on track for success.

Limiting Mindset #7: "No one believes in me, so why should I?"

With every new business I was excited to launch, I realized that fewer people in my community supported the journey.

When I created Garden In The Pines, I had hundreds of comments congratulating us, tons of new followers on my business page, and even a handful of initial orders. As time went on, my dad began to buy his flowers from the grocery store instead of from me because I was "too expensive for his taste."

As events were piling up and requiring more of my time, fewer people offered to help with the kids, even when I desperately needed a babysitter.

When I created my second business, Jersey Strike Co, I had a few comments and a couple follows from my Facebook friends, but the difference in number from my previous launch was significant.

When I created my podcast, maybe three people bothered to listen.

When I created my digital production agency, Mama Media, no one followed, shared, or inquired about our services.

With every new journey and burst of development personally and professionally, fewer people supported the journey. Fewer people shared with their friends, and not many even liked a post so that the social media algorithms could work their magic.

As I continued to develop myself, continued to grow in my

business, and continued accomplishing my goals, I realized that the lack of support had very little to do with other people's belief in my abilities. Instead, it had a lot more to do with their own feelings of inadequacy and insecurity as I continued to dominate my life.

- -

When you embark on your entrepreneurial journey, you might notice that the community of loved ones around you will not be supportive of your journey. There are so many reasons why your support system ceases being supportive, but many times it is because they simply do not understand what you're doing and why. Your family, your friends, and your community might not recognize you anymore as you evolve into the best version of yourself and make the shift to a confident mom-preneur. You truly are transforming into a new person as your mindset, actions, and choice of community evolves.

As you forge forward, the people that you once surrounded yourself with will understand you less and less. They won't understand your desire for growth and change, or why you are investing so much into this new adventure.

Accepting that the community of people that once embraced you will likely not purchase from your business is difficult, but necessary. They might not like or share your social media content or even ask about your progress. If they do ask, they may even wait for the opportunity to put down your ideas. Understand that this is simply a reflection of their own limiting beliefs or feelings of inadequacy.

Instead, learning how to pick out the people who fit into your new life is crucial to your growth and success. As you go on, you'll figure out who is worth speaking to, who will build you up and motivate you, and who you'd like to model yourself after. On the flip side, you'll discover who plays a toxic role in your life and stunts your ability to move forward. Entrepreneurship, especially mompreneurship, can be a lonely journey.

Surrounding yourself with a supportive community, full of like-minded people with similar goals, will help you to level up in your life and business. A supportive community will open your mind to new opportunities, solutions, and ideas for growth. This community will inspire you and give you the opportunity to connect with and inspire others that may be starting their journey, too.

Does this feel right to you? If so, I recommend joining communities through conferences, mastermind groups, group coaching programs, retreats, and even Facebook groups. If you do it right, each of these communities will have the people you need to empower you and help you overcome hardships in your business, personal life, and self-development.

Each of these communities will welcome you to the room, mama.

Phase 2: Mom Guilt, Thriving Within the Limits of Parenthood, and Overcoming Time Mismanagement

Moms can be happy, too. When I gave birth to my first, I felt defeated. Beyond the physical and emotional labors of a very difficult pregnancy, a traumatic delivery, and depressing postpartum, I had become detached and uninspired. I lost my connection with myself and where I saw my life going. As a woman, I felt that I had so much potential and could take on anything, but at the same time, felt a deep pull to disappear into my child's needs.

Don't get me wrong –it is so important as moms, especially at first, to turn all that attention towards the children to help them adjust to those first few months exploring the world. And of course, I always plan to be there for my kids as they grow, learn, and thrive. But is it really that selfish and disappointing for me to feel like I need something more?

Before I had baby number two, I took my wild ideas and ran with them. Still in the throes of navigating new parenthood, and expecting another baby soon, I launched myself into first-time business ownership. Looking back, I'm sure anyone would say that it was insane how much responsibility and stress I took on all at once, especially with very little experience. No matter what anyone

41

says or thinks, quitting my nine-to-five job cooped up in a windowless "office" to bet on myself was the best decision I ever made.

Why? I chose to fill up my own cup first. In doing so, I could actually give of myself more fully to everyone who needed me. I felt even more attached to my baby girl, ironically enough. *And* I was able to enjoy every moment with so much more joy, satisfaction, and peace.

So, how can you achieve this inner peace and reach your dreams? With time on your side, and your mindset helping to create solutions, we know that we can pursue your passions *now*. With the right time management strategies on your side, we can take inspired action to create the business that supports your ideas, passions, and lifestyle you've been longing for.

To do this, we first need to overcome some of the new challenges, limiting beliefs, and self-doubt that will wreak havoc in your mind as you begin putting an entrepreneurial plan in place. You may have the right mom-preneurial mindset, but now you need to face logistical challenges balancing motherhood and professional work. These hurdles create new doubts as you embark on this entrepreneurial journey. I'm ready to work with you so that you can confidently take action and make important decisions before we begin to implement the plan and establish your business.

In this next chapter, I want to discuss the limiting mindsets that I see so many moms get stuck on. These beliefs, mostly internalized from our culture, shame us out of ever reaching for anything outside of our assigned labels. All of these limiting mindsets really fit into one fat lie, repeated to us over and over by society and our inner voice: "How dare you have any free time in the day? You should be busy with chores, pleasing your spouse, and taking care of your kids." Let's take down mom guilt once and for all —and we can do this with the magic of time management!

Limiting Mindset #8: "How could I be spending time building a business when I should want to spend my free time with my kids?"

I should be playing with my kids, I thought, as I continued typing away on my computer. Over my keyboard clacking, I listened to them play in the living room. I dreaded looking up every few minutes because I knew I'd catch them looking up at me, hoping I would come join them soon.

I should be working on my to-do list, I thought, as I played with my kids. I couldn't help myself from glancing up at my computer, sitting on the couch just a few feet away, calling my name, begging me to be productive.

I shouldn't be working so hard because I am missing the most precious days of their lives, I thought, as I wrapped my last bouquet in my garage studio at 3 AM, prepping for an event in the early morning.

I should be making money for them, I thought, as I shopped through the grocery store with the girls in the cart's kiddy seats, doing mental math somersaults to figure out how many formula containers I could afford.

My kids are distracting me when I could be working on a large business proposal tonight, I thought, as I impatiently waited for my husband to come home from work.

I shouldn't go to the gym if I have so much work to accomplish today, I thought, going on my fifth day of sitting at a desk.

I should be cooking a nice meal for my family before it's too late, I thought, as I finished up a meeting with an important potential client.

Every contradicting thought possible would seep into my brain no matter the task at hand. If I was working, I thought of my kids. If I was with my kids, I thought of work. Each aspect of my life distracting me from the others, I never fully felt present in anything I did. Mom guilt made me feel like no matter what I was doing, it was wrong and I was a terrible mom.

Peace didn't come until I realized that everything is temporary. My current stage of life is only here for a few moments in the grand scheme of things, so whatever hard decisions I faced at this moment would no longer be a problem in the blink of an eye. While I focused on accomplishing big, forward-thinking goals, I reminded myself that my kids are well-cared for in the present. They are healthy, happy, and loved right now, and there's nothing wrong with me ensuring that I am healthy and happy right now, too. Not only that, but I was doing everything I needed and more to ensure that our future would be healthier and happier than it is in the present.

- -

As a mom, guilt seems to come with the title. You feel guilty for working because you're not around your family. When you're around your family, you feel guilty because you're not working. If you work from home, you feel guilty because you're not as productive with work and not as present with your kids.

You feel guilty for feeding them a quick and easy meal because you worked all day. You feel guilty for taking the time to make a home-cooked meal because you could've done more work with that time. You feel guilty for staying up late to work on the business because you lose the precious sleep you need to be alert and pleasant when taking care of your kids the next morning.

All of these guilty thoughts haven't even gone on to cover guilt over your spouse —the lost memories, laughs, conversations, date opportunities, and nights sleeping next to each other.

Motherhood is full of paradoxes. No matter which tasks and people we choose to spend time with, we'll always feel like we could have done something more, something better. We will always feel guilty about the decisions we make.

So, what's the only way to feel at ease with your decision-making processes?

Remember your vision each day. Multiple times per day. Your vision is your "why." It's the reason you're working your ass off in the first place. It's the reason you need to sacrifice time with your children, the self-care, the hobbies, and the family time you used to enjoy. It means a lot of sacrifices, but it also means creating the future that you envision for yourself, your kids, and your family.

The only way that the vision comes to fruition is by overcoming the mom guilt. You bring your vision to life by reminding yourself that this phase of hustle is temporary, and that building this business will be for your family's greater good.

Limiting Mindset #9: "Burnout, loneliness, lack of support, lack of sleep, no showers... Is it even worth it?"

My eye was twitching, and my furrowed brow was giving me a headache. From computer tab to computer tab, my internet browser looked like a window into my brain. It never turned off. An idea was never forgotten, it was simply bookmarked for a later date. Eighty-six tabs were open, and many of them were from the same website, just different pages.

My brain jumped from idea to idea, from task to task on my to-do list. It struggled to prioritize the most important item on the list because they all needed to get done, and they all felt urgent to me.

I was drained. I was tired. I was unhappy.

What was the point of being an entrepreneur to create your own schedule if you worked around the clock every day of the year?

Entrepreneurship was supposed to be a good thing for my family, my mindset, my financial situation, my fulfillment, and my growth. Instead, I had never felt more tired, more alone, or more unhappy.

My husband and I slept next to each other every single night, but we hadn't seen one another, had a date, or really connected in months.

Each day I got up, brought the kids to school and immediately dove into my to-do list on the computer. He got up and went to work so that we could support our lifestyle while I grew the business and made things happen.

I'm telling you the story of our business journey, but everything I'm saying is still our reality. We have a grand vision for the future for our family, and it's all on me to make it happen.

Every night, we fight for approximately ninety minutes to get the girls down for bed. We've officially entered the 'terrible twos' and it is definitely living up to the title. After a hundred trips to the bedroom, another five trips to the kitchen to get more milk, three trips to grab a snack, and a potty break or two, we finally retreated back to the computer desk to complete the original task we were working on.

My cup was empty. Sometimes, it still is.

Not my coffee cup, my personal energy cup. My energy for life. My motivation to get up every morning, and my patience to spread positivity to others. It's empty.

My brain is swimming constantly with a running to-do list of items for my business, my kids, my finances, my meager excuse for a social life, and any upcoming events that family asks us to attend. I'm constantly trying to reprioritize the list, scrambling to figure out how I can squeeze in some quiet time for myself, too.

How am I supposed to show up for anything when my cup is empty? There's nothing to give.

In order to give myself to others, I first need to give myself the respect, love, and support I need to feel full.

- -

As mom-preneurs, we are constantly giving to everyone around us.

We are giving to our kids, our partners, our siblings, our friends, our pets, our business, our clients, and we're the last thing on the list. When everyone else requires so much, there's nothing left in the cup for us.

Do this day-in and day-out, and you'll find that you're brutally exhausted, drained, and unhappy. You're not fulfilled.

When we move ourselves to the top of the list, we give ourselves the space we need to grow and develop personally. Once we take care of ourselves, we can move on to take care of everyone else around us in a better way. Ever heard of putting on your oxygen mask before you help others?

As entrepreneurs, our clients can sense our energy. They can feel when we're abundant and they can feel when we're empty.

Clients that are receiving the empty version of ourselves aren't receiving the highest quality of work. When our cups are empty, we are just trying to fulfill the contract with no love for the work we're doing.

When our cup is full, when we take care of ourselves first, we're able to perform our job better. We're able to grow our business, dedicate the mental space to problem solve, and attract everything we want in our life toward us.

When we're happy, everyone around us is happy, including our clients.

Here's what that looks like: Make it an intention to take care of yourself by scheduling your personal time into the calendar. In doing this, you make it a priority to fill up your cup each day. In the morning, you will be fulfilled, energized, and ready to move on to the rest of your day.

You'll have the feeling of productivity because you accomplished all of those self-care tasks in the morning. In addition, you'll no longer have to worry about taking care of your self-care items, so you have the brain space to conquer the rest of the day. You can fully show up for everyone else because you are not resentful, frustrated, or exhausted. You're not wondering all day how you'll be able to squeeze in that hour at the gym or finally take a shower.

Now, you're using your time more intentionally for self-care, and that means you're much less likely to get sucked into brain-drain behaviors that are a reaction to complete burnout (*hello Instagram*).

Scheduling intentional time each morning into your calendar on a daily basis sets you up for success. It gives you the brain space to grow, feel fulfilled, and ultimately fill your cup so that it can flow unto those around you in your life and your business.

Limiting Mindset #10: "I don't have the time."

My newborn only wanted me to hold her, and since she was just diagnosed with RSV, I was terrified of leaving her alone.

Every couple of minutes, she would stop breathing. In the sweetest of dreams, in the deepest newborn sleep, she would startle awake to cough uncontrollably to the point of losing her breath. No air would pass through her mouth for what felt like the longest fifteen seconds I've ever experienced. The only thing I could do to get relief was to keep her close under my watch. That way, I could act quickly if it seemed to take too long for her to catch her breath.

So, we worked together. The business was my baby, too. I was determined to somehow make them both healthy, strong, and resilient.

My newborn would lie nuzzled in my arm while I sat in my rocking chair, which I had pulled up to my desktop. I ran my mouse along the side of my leg and tapped the keyboard keys on top of my lap. My word per minute speed had been decimated as I could only type away on the keyboard one letter at a time. Thankfully, she slept most of that time that we worked together. I figured that, even if I was working a bit slower than normal, I would still be moving the needle forward in my business.

It was usually 2 AM when we would finally make it upstairs to bed. Four hours was usually enough time, I discovered, to feel rested enough for the next day. I always said a prayer that my almost-two-year-old would barge into my room no earlier than 6 AM. I drifted to sleep, knowing I would do it all over again the next day.

Each morning, my newborn and I would wake to face another days' work.

Together, we have created my email workflows and automations. We have done them and redone them. We've moved those workflows over to different platforms every time I changed my mind. We've created offers of freebies and opt-ins to begin growing our email list, and we've created designs for our wedding clients to help them envision their wedding day decor. We created my first course together. We changed that course and moved onto other projects together. We attended virtual mastermind meetings together. We attended coaching meetings together. She truly is the most experienced newborn I've ever met.

I used to think that there was never going to be time for me to grow this business as a mom.

I used to think that there was never enough time in the day as a mom for anything, let alone entrepreneurship. The to-do list never ended, so how was it all going to get done if I needed eight hours of sleep at night, too?

I used to think that everything needed to be put on hold until the kids were in school, or graduated and out on their own.

I used to think that, in the busiest of seasons, I needed to wait to start a new project until a slow season in my life.

While some of these thoughts had some truth to them, I needed to look harder at my attitude and intentions. Did I really not have *any* time in the day for anything? Did I really need *tons* of free time available to start a new project or take care of myself?

How intentionally was I using the time I had every day? Did motherhood really cancel out any opportunities to be and do anything else?

While my child was a newborn, I was able to move the needle by working with my child's needs in mind. I knew she would sleep a lot at her age, and that she would sleep better in my arms. I also knew I needed to keep a close eye on her. Motherhood means constantly evolving and learning, being flexible with your child's stage of development, so I was always reworking my strategy for getting things done.

As ironic as it sounds, her newborn stage was actually the easiest for getting things done. Once she grew out of my arms, I realized that I had to structure my day differently. At first, my day looked a little something like this:

TIME MISMANAGEMENT SCHEDULE

6AM-8AM	I got the kids up and dressed, then we snuggled in bed
8AM - 8:30AM	I brought the kids to daycare
8:30AM - 9AM	I tidied up the house
9:30AM -11AM	my morning workout at the gym
11AM - 11:20AM	cooling down from the gym, I'd sit on my phone, getting distracted
11:20AM - 12:00 PM	I'd eat for the first time and get sucked into my phone some more
12PM - 12:15PM	finally, some productive work
12:15PM - 12:45PM	brain break... I get sucked into my phone even more
1PM -1:30PM	more productive work
1:30PM - 3PM	attend some meetings
3:15PM - 3:45PM	cooling down from talking to people, I get sucked into my phone
3:45PM - 4:15PM	more productive work
3:45PM - 4:15PM	more productive work
4:30PM - 4:45PM	time to get kids from daycare
4:45PM - 6:30PM	I'd play on my phone while the kids played
7PM	the kids' bedtime
8PM - BED	TV time before bed

Did you see a pattern? I wasted too much time on my phone, interrupting the time that I could be spending with my kids after school, being productive, or working on a passion project.

When I sat down and wrote out how I spent my time, minute to minute, I realized that there actually was plenty of time in the day. Instead of limiting myself by thinking I was too busy to do anything, I just needed to manage my time better and eliminate my distractions.

- -

Time slips from the hourglass as the kids need to be dressed, laundry needs to be swapped, school buses are pulling up honking, and breakfast is burning in the kitchen. Your timeclock at work has never seen an "on time" stamp because time never seems to be on your side. How can you manage a business on top of this already too-hectic life?

As a mom, you've never seen your schedule this full. Juggling this many balls seems impossible, especially when even taking a shower is often in question.

Being a mom is a full-time job already, especially in the midst of newborn, toddler, and pre-school stages. If you're a work-from-home mom like me, you understand even more deeply how overwhelmed you can be when society deems YOU responsible for both domestic life *and* professional life. It's really like you have three full-time jobs –childcare, maid, and entrepreneur –so you feel like you should have three separate time clocks, not just one.

All moms suffer under this weight of responsibility, but how can you differentiate yourself as a mom that does it all? How can you step away from being that mom that never has enough time in the day?

Understand that you have the power to create momentum in your business and work through challenges. You are strong, you are capable. Believe that you *do* have the time, then find that time in your schedule. Take control of the chaos and set it straight. That is the key differentiator.

Mismanagement of time is the fatal flaw of unsuccessful mompreneurs.

Raising kids, tending to the house, supporting your partner, working, and building a business from the ground up is a lot to manage. Of course you are busy –honestly, too busy. There's nothing wrong with admitting that. There's no shame in admitting that you feel crushed under all these tasks and burned out at the end of every day.

But, have you taken a hard look at exactly how you spend your time?

When you're working, are you actually working? Or are you working for only a few minutes before you're sucked into a death scroll on TikTok for 45 minutes? Do you find yourself finally getting into a zone at work five minutes before the baby starts screaming to be fed again?

Be honest with yourself, because that will be your ticket to finding solutions. Moms everywhere are struggling with these limitations. Understanding your limitations is the first step to restructuring your life so that you can begin moving the needle on your business. You'll be able to create solutions for your lack of productivity, and you'll finally start creating more momentum as you accomplish your goals.

Once you've written down which distractions suck your time –the TV, your phone, minor unfinished chores, self-care tasks, etc. –you can completely cut them out or dedicate time in your schedule for taking care of those things. Doing this will help you create pockets of undistracted focus time for productive work.

Dedicating a small block of undistracted time to a productive task actually provides you with far more results than an abundance of distracted, unstructured time.

Productive time creates the brainspace you need to work on all of the items you want to accomplish in a day. When time is used intentionally, it actually seems to multiply. Suddenly, you're able to carve out time for work, for kids, for chores, and still have the time left over to social scroll.

Sitting down to write out a schedule doesn't just help you find your common distractions. This practice can also help you find patterns in your day. For example, if your undistracted time is to be used for tending to your children, you'll be able to find time in your day when they are usually occupied or not home. In those pockets of "childless" time, you're able to dedicate your leftover focus time to other productive tasks like your business growth.

Let me tell you, it blew my mind when I realized that the time was there, that I was just using it wrong. My mindset concerning the concept of time completely changed. This discovery made me question everything I was doing and consider which tasks were really a valuable use of my time. It made me constantly ask the question, "How can I create intentional focus time today?"

Asking yourself these questions about the value of your time helps put daily tasks into perspective. You start wondering which tasks are worth your time, and which tasks would be better done by someone else, put off until later, or not done at all. Some tasks that give you the illusion of being productive might not be productive at all, but instead are a time-suck taking away from more valuable tasks. Ask yourself, is this task helping me achieve a goal of mine, or helping me become a better version of myself? Is it helping me move the needle on my life, personally or professionally?

Here are five of my favorite ways to maximize my time and productivity:

1. Create a block schedule.

    Block scheduling is a concept that encourages you to block out time on your calendar, each block stating between three and five intentions for that time. The block is usually about three hours long, and it gives you the flexibility to move tasks around in that block without cluttering your calenda. like a typical appointment calendar might.

    Creating blocks dedicated to different areas of your life helps you to be more productive. Bonus: it helps you break down mom-guilt you may be experiencing because you can point right to a block of time on your calendar when you were present and intentional with your kids.

Side Note: I want to be clear that the issue isn't lack of time with your kids —moms know they spend their entire day thinking, breathing, and living motherhood. Instead, it's that you're not spending enough *quality time* with your kids. Please, put the dang phone away. I intentionally hide it from myself. That way, your kids feel that you're present, and you feel present. Your phone can no longer be a habit when it's tucked away, and you'll feel much better about your kid-time.

2. Purchase a timer.

    You might feel like this is excessive at first, but don't knock it until you try it. Utilizing a timer when working on select tasks helps you be more productive with the work you do in that time frame. You can combine this with your block scheduling to help you pace the tasks you've dedicated to that block, too.

    For example, if I give myself one hour to record five quick YouTube videos, it gets done in an hour every time. If I gave myself three hours, I usually allow myself the three hours to get it done, meaning I'm much less productive and I've lost two more hours of my day.

    Give yourself intentional deadlines to see the needle move quicker.

3. Intentionally hide your distractions.

    I talked about this when it came to quality time with your kids, but it really needs to be your practice all day long if you're serious about time management. My favorite thing to do is throw my phone across the room when I am working on my computer. My phone has a habit of calling my name when it's sitting within reach. I can't help myself from checking to see if someone interacted with a post, sent me a text, or DM'ed me on Instagram. Removing the possibility of being distracted by tossing the phone across the room helps to reinforce my intentional time blocks and stick with my timer.

4. Create a to-do list.

    If you don't know what you need to accomplish, or if you have to think for even a few seconds about it, you lose the momentum and motivation. Keep the momentum flowing by having a ready-made to-do list sitting out on the desk or stuck to your fridge. Every morning, you can check it and update it, then refer to it throughout the day in blocks that you've dedicated to that list. It's so much easier to be intentional about the tasks for the day when they are staring you in the face. You can't make the excuse that you forgot. This also helps you feel settled and focused on the tasks at hand for a specific time block, because you've freed up the brainspace that previously had been distracted by always thinking about things you need to do. That way, the list helps keep you productive and moving forward toward your goals.

5. Carve out time in the calendar for you-time.

    Just like the to-do list can help you free up brainspace, carving out self-care time in your calendar helps you feel at ease. You don't have to obsess about when you'll take that shower, get that haircut, go on a date with your spouse, because it has already been settled. You'll also feel much better when you've taken the time to care for yourself. You need to keep that cup full!

This is going to be the hardest time management hack to accomplish because everything else seems to be a bigger priority. But if you are not well-rested and fulfilled, you are going to be impatient, resentful, and unhappy as you work to pursue your passion. Carve out the time each morning, pencil it into your calendar, and fill your cup first so that the rest of your day is spent overflowing with love, passion, and support.

Time management is not a superpower. It's the skill of knowing yourself so well that you intentionally remove the distractions from your life. It's the ability to question everything you're doing so you know that it's a productive use of your time (for joy or for your goals). The supermoms that have mastered time management will move mountains when others only thought they could climb them.

Phase 3: Mama Has a Vision.

Having a vision for your success is important for your journey as a mom-preneur. The vision will help inform every decision you make. It will remind you what you're working toward, keep you on target for growth, and help you surround yourself with like-minded people —not necessarily the people related to you by blood, that you roomed with in college, or that grew up down the street from you, but the people that lift you up, support you, and guide you as you achieve your ideal life and business.

Creating your vision and reminding yourself of it constantly will be the fuel to your fire as you develop your business plan. It's important to keep it in mind throughout every step of the process, as it will help you create a business that aligns with your strengths, joys, passions, and ideal customer.

When you have a business plan that so perfectly aligns with you, operating it will come so naturally that it will surprise you. You'll also create a strong marketing plan because you'll believe in your idea and know it intimately in your core.

With renewed passion, self-confidence, self-care, and time management mastery, you can feel confident in starting to plan the business. You have the mom-preneur mindset and the tools to take control of your life; now it's time to start putting your vision to paper.

To do this, we need to find your niche so you can stand out in the crowd. We need to create your marketing plan to communicate pure value to your ideal customer. We need to find the room of supporters that will welcome you on the journey of growth. As you close in on implementing your vision, we need to discuss choosing the right tools to create flow and communicating like a professional with a well-oiled process.

Throughout the course of this chapter, you'll read about my mistakes as a new entrepreneur trying to develop new businesses. Each limiting mindset that I encountered will align with a new task you need to complete on your journey of fast-tracking your business building. In your workbook, I recommend that you complete the action items as we work through each mindset barrier together. That way, you'll feel empowered to move the needle towards turning your vision into an actual operating business.

Limiting Mindset #11: "There's no room for me."

When I began my floral design business, I used to think that every business existed and operated alone, and that every business owner made decisions only for their own profit. Each time an inquiry came through the door, I imagined every local florist was chomping at the bit to out-bid the other proposals.

That was business, right? It's a dog-eat-dog world out there, sharks are in the water and you have to fend for yourself. Out-do the competition at every turn.

It wasn't until I unexpectedly received three referrals for weddings from a local florist that my mindset was challenged.

Why would she do that?

Once you enter into a true business perspective as an entrepreneur, you realize that business operates a whole lot different than you thought. As a customer, you wouldn't think about how a business might have reasons to turn away a potential customer. It hadn't crossed my mind before that maybe she was already booked for that date, that the client's style didn't align with her style, or that their personalities just weren't a match.

I am a competitor to my core. I am an achiever. To me, everything is a competition. When I experienced a competitor sending me a lead in goodwill, it completely shook my view of the business world.

I began to realize that there is more power in community than in competition.

Ironically, the majority of referrals I receive are from other "competing" florists. Not planners, photographers, or venues, but what I used to consider my competition.

My "competition" actually had a lot of reasons to pass on inquiries. Florists are artists, so the styles, color palettes, venues, and blooms they prefer to work with often inform which clients they choose. They're also typically small local businesses, so they're limited in the number of weddings they can book as well as the size and location of those weddings. As with most other service-based businesses that enter into long-term high-stakes contracts, florists also need to make sure that their clients are a good personality match. Other florists began flooding me with inquiries that they chose to pass on for whatever reason, especially when I began offering unique services that couldn't be found elsewhere.

By spreading the wealth to the community rather than hoarding it (which would likely result in underdelivering on those contracts), the florist community was more successful overall. We'd be able to expand the abilities of each other's businesses by sharing our rental items for events instead of everyone purchasing their own rental items for just one use. We could pair up to place bulk orders so that we could all reduce operating expenses. We could even share our favorite tools and tricks if we were feeling extra chummy.

By fostering relationships with other florists, I was actually able to get myself more referrals from other florists. My business was at top-of-mind for them when a client asked for a service they didn't offer, a date they didn't have open, or a style that didn't align.

Ultimately, at the root of my fierce competitive attitude was a deep-seated fear of scarcity.

When I realized that there was more than enough business to go around, I was able to let go of that fear. We can all help one another thrive. That significant change in mindset caused my business to soar.

- -

Have you ever walked into a space and felt like you didn't belong? That there were too many other *better* people in the room, so why try?

The funny thing about that self-deprecating thought is that it likely comes from a competitive scarcity mindset. You believe that these people are your competition, not your community, and that you are all pitted against each other for a limited amount of resources. You're likely thinking, *these people are better than me, so they're going to get the client* instead of thinking, *I have a unique value that I can provide, but that prospect might not align with my business. If that other business doesn't feel like they align with the client, they'll be able to refer me instead.*

Connecting with peers in your industry is powerful and enlightening. It gives you the ability to receive relatable advice, feedback, recommended tools, shared equipment and supplies, and even a helping hand. Together, you can probem-solve so that everyone can thrive, like deciding to place bulk orders, creating a room that's safe for venting, and helping each other refine and achieve goals.

The biggest benefit of all is that there is enough business to go around, but you'll only get a chance at that business if everyone shares it with everyone else. There is more business to be had than anyone can handle on their own, and there is an abundance of resources that are better shared than hoarded.

After all, each business owner has unique ideas, lessons learned, and life-changing experiences. You tell me –is it better that you only ever operate based on your own ideas and mistakes, or make decisions informed by a community that shares their mistakes, regrets, successes, and innovations?

With the new idea of community in mind, you will see exponential growth in your business. You'll be able to avoid mistakes by learning from others, build each other up with shared resources, and still differentiate yourself by offering unique values, personality traits, and strengths.

That scared, competitive business owner that walked into a room of competitors is going to now embrace that room full of support and abundance. You're going to feel like you can conquer anything in front of you, and that you really do have the power to do anything you want in this life.

Limiting Mindset #12: "No one will ever find my business in the crowd."

When creating my floral design business, I did a quick search on wedding advertising platforms to gauge how many other florists were in my area. A brief search yielded over three hundred businesses, and I knew they weren't all advertising on these platforms.

The feeling of being a needle in the haystack washed over me. There are so many similar businesses out there, so how would anyone even find me? How could I expose people to my business in a way that actually won attention and drew in couples that were my ideal clients?

As I began my brainstorming process, I realized that I needed to be very specific about the audience I wanted to serve. Yes, wedding couples. But there are millions of people living in New Jersey and I didn't want to work with *all* of them. I narrowed it down: I only wanted to work with the couples that value me, my ideas, and who light me up during our sessions.

I broke out my journal and detailed my vision for the future, all of my unique qualities as a florist and business owner, and I detailed my strengths and my weaknesses.

Here's what I wrote:

My Mission:
At Garden In The Pines, our goal is to turn your beautiful wedding/event dream into a cherished memory.

My Vision:
Garden In The Pines is an all-encompassing outdoor event venue and design team dedicated to transforming your dreams into a cherished memory.

My Brand Values:
Creativity
Passion
Natural Beauty
Sustainability
Superior Communication
Unmatched Professionalism

My Ideal Customer:
The elegant, upscale bride willing to invest in beautiful design and a seamless experience.

My Strengths:
Customer Service
Communication
Organization
Technology
Creativity
Thoughtfulness
Vision

My Weaknesses:
Perfectionism
Enneagram Three - The Competitive Overachiever
Indecisive at times
Needs reassurance
Always questioning if I am doing the right thing

By outlining all of this information, I was able to evaluate myself honestly and create a business marketing plan that aligned with my goals. I was able to create a vision and plan that worked best for my target audience, mission, and vision for my business. In addition, I was able to get ahead of my weakness by putting solutions in place and building a business that played to my strengths.

Most importantly, I was able to identify who I wanted to serve, why we would be uniquely aligned to work together, and how I could best communicate with them in my future marketing endeavors.

- -

When coming up with an idea for your business, there are several key things that you need to keep in mind. Take a minute to write these questions down and answer them:

1. Identify your soul-led passions.
2. Who is your target audience?
3. What problems do they have?
4. How are you going to solve those problems?

By answering these questions in great detail, you will be able to create a business that is true to your strengths and serves your audience well.

Specifically, you'll be able to narrow down your audience from *everyone* to just a few really great matches. As the saying goes, "Niches get riches."

But what is a niche?

A niche is a specific subset of an audience for a particular product or service. When you think about the types of people in the world, there are millions that fall within each category: male, female, kids, teenagers, elderly, middle-aged, entrepreneurs, coaches, nutritionists, chefs, and so on. You'll need to pick categories and subcategories to the point that you are identifying exactly who you want to walk through your door.

For your business plan, it's best to go through the below exercise to help you identify your niche. The more specific you are, the better.

A. Identify your soul-led passion.

Brain dump everything that brings you joy onto the journal page. You're going to be talking about this a lot as you build and grow your business, so it's important that you are truly passionate about the topic.

Remember, you are going to be living, breathing, and thinking about this topic day-after-day, and working in the beginning even when it's not making money. Identify what you'd be willing to do for free, because you won't be seeing any paychecks any time soon.

B. Identify your target audience.

Create a customer avatar that is in perfect alignment with your product or service. In other words, you need to think of what your audience's "mascot" would be, such as "Nancy from the upper-class neighborhood who takes her kids to soccer practice after school, knits on the weekends, and is obsessed with daytime soap operas."

I encourage you to be as detailed as possible. Identify where they shop, what they buy, what their friend groups look like, the types of jobs they work, and everything in between. The more detailed you are about this person, the easier it will be for you to build your business to serve this person.

    C. Identify the problems that your target audience may be experiencing.

It's most valuable to survey your target audience so that you can gather actual data and insight. If you can't then do your research online so that you can identify their common issues and what kind of solutions they need. Suddenly, you know exactly what kind of product or service you can create to sell to your ideal customer.

If you decide to ask your ideal audience directly, here are some common questions to use in your survey:

- What do you enjoy about _____?
- What problems are you experiencing related to _____?
- If you could waive a magic wand to solve _____, what would that magic wand do?
- Does price influence your decision to solve this problem?
- What price point feels best to solve this problem for you?
- What would be the best solution to solve this problem for you?
    - Done-for-you service?
    - DIY solution with the knowledge and steps?
    - 1:1 program?
    - Group program?
    - Product?

- o A combination of these?
- Does this solution already exist? If so, what is it missing?
- Does timing influence when you'd purchase this solution, such as holidays or seasons?
- If I created this for you to solve your problem, would you purchase this service from me?

Surveys like this really do all the work for you. Getting valuable data from your aligned audience helps you to time your launch perfectly, get your messaging correct, and improve upon existing solutions that have failed them in the past.

D. Identify how you are different from your competition.

It's best to do some research about your industry peers in your area or online. Identify their branding, who they are serving, and what they're advertising to their audience so that you can solve the need even better for your target audience.

Completing the steps above will also help you to dial in your branding, messaging, and product or service to fill any gaps in the industry.

Niching down your business might seem like limiting yourself, but it's actually helping you profit more from the customers that matter the most. You also will never be in direct competition with those "competitors," as you won't be looking for the same clients. Even better, you'll be at the forefront of their mind when they encounter the exact customers they know you serve best.

Limiting Mindset #13: "I'll never find my first client."

In trying to build a floral design business with no experience, reputation in the industry, or anything to call a portfolio, I had a difficult time finding clients to work with me.

The thing about starting a business and building a clientele from the ground up is that it means you have to get back to the basics of marketing. But first, I had to understand marketing.

I read dozens of books about the concept of marketing, but many were too textbook-like to sink in. I needed actionable steps and real-life examples to begin pulling in leads and making sales.

One of the simplest and most easily comprehensible definitions I've ever read about marketing is outlined in the book, *The One Page Marketing Plan* by Allen Dib. It read:

> If the circus was coming, and you went looking for a site to pitch the 'Big Top', that's market research.

> If you painted a sign before the circus came to town announcing, "Circus Coming to Town on Saturday!", that's advertising.

> If you put your sign on the back of an elephant and marched it through town, that's promotion.

> If the elephant, still with the sign on his back, tramples through the mayor's garden, and it makes the evening news, that's publicity.

If you get the mayor to laugh about it, that's public relations.

If you deliberately lead the elephant past schools and through residential neighborhoods, that's market segmentation.

When town's residents come to your circus and you show them the array of games, treats and entertainment stalls, explain how much fun they'll have enjoying the circus performers, answer their questions about the attractions and, ultimately, they spend their hard earned money at your circus, that's sales.

If you created, planned and managed all these activities, that's MARKETING![1]

This analogy was simple, but it outlined all of the concepts necessary for a complete understanding of marketing. It helped me envision what marketing would look like in practice, not just its definitions on paper. Thank God, it finally slapped me in the face.

While I could have big ideas about grand marketing gestures, I still had no experience putting pen to paper for a strong marketing plan. My situation's urgency required a quick and successful orchestration of leads and sales, so I really couldn't waste two more years trying to learn how to create a marketing plan for myself.

Against my usual instinct to "save money" by doing everything myself, I hired a marketing expert to help me set my business straight.

"It's five thousand dollars for my ninety-day marketing program." This expert was sure to help me set my business straight. If I made the investments now in this first year of business, I assured myself that I would shave off years of mistakes and revisions so that I could achieve my goals faster and with less struggle.

Our strategy was to connect with other vendors, like planners, photographers, and venues, to build a fruitful network of referrals. In addition, I needed to revamp my website so that my business would look more professional and attract the ideal client for my goals. Of course, this also meant that essentially my entire brand would have to evolve, because my original attempt spoke to a broad audience and attracted more low-budget, non-wedding clients.

We began our work together with a complete deep dive into my brand, my current business structure, process for bookings, setup of automations and emails, copy on my website, posts on social media channels, and all of my client materials. With each close look, we needed to ensure that we were consistently communicating my brand's unique values, style, and personality.

We had also begun researching brand designers and website developers to refresh my business image across the board. We wanted the image to be cohesive, clear, and aligned with what my ideal clients would enjoy.

Each week, I had homework of my own to accomplish so that we stayed on target with our timeline —wedding season was quickly approaching.

Inquiries come in waves in my industry, so I made it a priority to get my branding on point as early in the year as possible. That way, I was prepared for the next wave of inquiries to come through.

In the course of our deep dive, we discovered some aspects of my business that should be a priority when advertising. These aspects would actually yield a greater profit margin and would help ease other common margin issues associated with weddings and events. When we hired my website and brand designer, we emphasized these aspects in our discussions to make sure the more profitable arms of my business would be advertised boldly and clearly.

The work we put in as a team over the course of our ninety days together helped lay a solid foundation for business going forward. My marketing mentor gave me the ability to create a marketing plan each quarter. She also helped establish a solid brand that would help communicate my business's core values and grow with my business as I leveled up each year.

- -

Marketing is one of the most important aspects of your business – without it, word-of-mouth is just about the only way anyone will ever find you… and if you're new, I wouldn't necessarily count on word-of-mouth. If you don't have leads from your marketing efforts, you won't have the potential for sales conversations, and if you don't have sales conversations, you won't have clients. Without clients, well, you get the point.

In the social media era, we often think that simply posting on Instagram or Facebook will immediately create a business for us. It's the only marketing that most young entrepreneurs engage in because, well, it's just what we're familiar with. We think that a few beautifully designed posts will bring clients clammering at our door. This confidence might be bolstered even more by a large personal following that tended to give us significant engagement in the past. I hate to burst your bubble, but your following liked your posts because they enjoyed seeing *you*. When it comes to a business venture, that previously-reliable following might not be as interested.

As a mom-preneur, we see other moms on social media killing it with their business promotion, and their families appear to be thriving. My family has had a bowl of cheerios with a side of graham crackers for dinner every night this week.

They have large audiences and big followings. It appears that they have all of the engagement in the world. My posts go out consistently, but it feels like it is taking forever to get followers, and even longer for those followers to engage.

These moms on social media appear to have brand deals and coaching businesses. They appear to get everything they want and reach every goal they set. How is it that I can't get my business to book high-value clients who respect my efforts, process, and beautiful arrangements?

So how do these successful mom-preneurs do it all?

The simple answer is that social media doesn't share the whole story. I see the highlight reel of every perfectly edited and curated life, propped up with filters and camera tricks. These accounts aren't really people, they're brands. They control the narrative and other people's perspectives so that they can market their service, affiliates, and show off their success. They've mastered the art of marketing.

Marketing can be a difficult beast without the right experience. It's also certainly not kind to those who haven't nailed the right messaging, branding, aesthetic, budget, team, testimonials, or clients!

The idea of a marketing plan scared me, so you shouldn't feel bad for hesitating, either. I kept feeling the pangs of imposter syndrome because I didn't have a marketing team to help me or any experience in marketing a business before. I'm sure you feel the same, but it doesn't have to be scary or difficult.

The marketing plan helps to ensure that you're setting the right intentions for that quarter. It helps you ensure that your intentions in marketing align with your business goals and mission statement. All of this sums up to moving the needle forward in your business.

Your marketing plan is a tool that you should revisit and re-create quarterly at a minimum. Think at least ninety days ahead of the schedule.

Each quarter has a new season of holidays, occasions, and gatherings. Many businesses plan their sales, promotions, and launches around these special occasions. Thinking of the year in sections will help you to better focus on specific opportunities rather than being overwhelmed. You can also choose to have a yearly marketing plan on top of your quarterlies, which helps you plan more long-term marketing campaigns to reach bigger goals.

Let's break down the components of a marketing plan so that you're best equipped to create one for yourself each quarter.

1. Key Information

The key information section of your marketing plan consists of your brand mission statement, vision, values, and ideal customer.

Make sure to utilize the customer avatar that you've created as you align your marketing plans with your business goals for the year or quarter. As you come up with marketing plans, you'll always be able to check them against this section to make sure you're actually taking actions that will help you reach your goals.

This section also helps you regularly revisit your "why" so that you can stay focused and motivated.

2. Marketing Initiatives

Your marketing initiatives will help you to outline exactly what needs to happen over the course of your marketing efforts to help you achieve your goals. In other words, the initiatives are the specific strategies that we are going to use.

For example, one of my goals in my marketing plan was to book five new clients this quarter.

Two initiatives that I wrote down to accomplish that goal were:

- Post daily on Instagram, Pinterest, and Facebook
- Make relationships with five new professional vendors in the industry

Both of these initiatives are challenging, but not impossible. In turn, they would help you take action toward bringing five clients into your business in that quarter without causing you to burn out or give up.

3. Specifics.

This is where it gets fun. The specifics break down the initiatives further so that you end up with a to-do list for your marketing campaign. You need to be as detailed as possible in the *how* of accomplishing the goals and initiatives.

For example, you would create:

- A list of tasks and a deadline for each task
- The messaging you aim to use
- Channels that you plan to utilize
- Assets you can use for that initiative
- How you will measure your success

Each of these specific details helps you to outline your step-by-step process so that your huge vision turns into less overwhelming actionable steps. You go from knowing you need to do *something* to knowing exactly what you need to do.

4. Due Dates.

At the end of your marketing plan, it is handy to include a section for all of your due dates and the tasks that need to be completed by those dates for easy reference. Organize it in the way that makes most sense to you and helps keep you motivated. It could be a calendar of monthly, weekly, or daily tasks. It could be an appointment style or a block style. Get creative and use your knowledge about your own strengths and weaknesses.

Your marketing plan is going to be your most important resource in your business. Without a marketing strategy and the actions you take to follow through, your business will be stagnant with no leads!

And you know what we don't have if we don't have leads...

Limiting Mindset #14: "It's going to take too long to get this business growing."

As a new entrepreneur with no experience owning and operating my business, I knew that I didn't want to waste years trying to figure the whole "business thing" out. I wanted to quickly earn revenue in my business by leveraging other people's audiences, gifts, and hard-learned lessons.

In all of the my favorite podcasts, books, and coaching sessions, I kept hearing this phrase over and over again: "Get in the room."

It was explained to me constantly that I needed to find the people who would help me level up. They would support and encourage growth in myself and my business. I needed to surround myself with people that were further ahead in the journey than me so I could learn from them and be inspired by them.

And if I couldn't join the room, then I needed to *create the room.*

In developing my fourth business, which was my personal brand, I knew that I needed to surround myself with other mom-preneurs that were doing the same thing. At the same time, they needed to be further ahead in the journey than me so that they could not only empathize, but also actually offer helpful advice. I wanted to learn about how they grew their audience quickly, their favorite tools and resources, and how they marketed their business. Bonus points –I needed to know how they were doing everything while raising kids.

While I knew that conferences were a huge step in networking and learning from experts, they were a heavy investment that I wasn't too sure I could afford. With four startups, I did not have the extra money budgeted towards networking.

Instead, I decided to host an online event. I invited twenty-eight women to join me in a virtual interview series that could be distributed to all of our audiences. We connected over Zoom to talk about all kinds of topics, from motherhood to entrepreneurship. I created the room of entrepreneurs that I wanted to be around and that I could learn from, and I decided to share it with everyone else, too.

- -

Have you heard the saying that you need to "get in the room?"

The idea stems from the fact that there are different archetypes of people all over the world. It builds on the fact that people that have similar personality types, ambitions, and accomplishments to your own are the people that will encourage self-growth without introducing detrimental adversity.

I like to put it this way: "You become who you surround yourself with." Surrounding yourself with people who have accomplished your goals or are several steps ahead of you toward accomplishing those common goals are the people that will motivate you to move forward. They can also help shave off years of hard-learned lessons if they're willing to share their knowledge with you.

Surrounding yourself with people that no longer support your goals, ambitions, or vision will encourage your limiting beliefs to reappear. You'll feel stuck in place, question your vision, and become unmotivated. However, surrounding yourself with people that light you up, inspire new ideas, and help solve issues you're experiencing as you grow your business will fast-track your path to success.

Creating your room often requires an investment of both time and money. You can create your room by joining mastermind groups with other elite professionals, attending conferences and local business networking events, or participating in virtual summits.

The other way to create your room –which I actually recommend even more –would be to physically host the event that will bring aligned people into your sphere. This choice could be as simple as organizing an event in your local library, restaurant, or hotel conference room. You can create a large-scale in-person event or an online event.

Regardless of the final product, becoming the host of the event suddenly elevates your status and helps you to become a peer to the elite professionals you invite. They'll see your event as valuable because it gives them a platform to communicate their benefits, and the value for you manifests as a platform to showcase your new elite status. You'll also be able to build authority as you share your learned experiences and offer to serve others in the group.

I'll give you an example. If you choose to host an online event, you could give other experts a chance to showcase their expertise through a lesson or interview to a shared audience. At the same time, you're building a relationship with them, showcasing your own expertise, and exposing your brand to their audience. An ideal outcome would be to grow your audience by reaching out to their similar audience, to reach new people through marketing the event, and to build your network of professionals who can support and motivate you on your journey.

Creating the network, or "room," of professionals who are aligned with your vision and goals will be your ticket to creating fast results in your business. Learn from their mistakes, get an inside look at their best-kept secrets, and reach new levels of growth that you never thought were possible.

Limiting Mindset #15: "I'm never going to break out of the work-to-survive cycle."

When I envisioned building my business, I had a vision of what success would look like when I hit my income goals. It would look like my family enjoying all our vacations, spending quality time together on a regular basis, never worrying about what we could afford at the grocery store. I saw all of the fruits of my labor paying off.

I didn't expect the reality of building a business from scratch. I didn't envision getting sucked into a work-to-survive cycle, where labor and exhaustion were all-consuming.

The reality of building a business on my own manifested as needing a list of babysitters so that I could keep calling one after the other for emergencies until someone finally came through. It was needing to stay up all hours of the night to complete tasks because no one else was going to do it for me. It was an endless string of emails after emails and calls after calls.

It looked like a day full of meetings on top of hours spent on content creation, podcast appearances, and planning. It looked like pretending I could complete tasks I had no business attempting like bookkeeping and website designing.

What really did it for me, though, was that it looked like working every single weekend and all the nights leading up to an event in order to fulfill our contracts because it was *my business*, and who else was going to do the work?

Of course, this was shortsighted –in the wedding floral industry, that would actually mean I worked every day and every night for the rest of my life. My reality was not sustainable, and it needed to be completely turned upside down. I needed to create a roster of happy clients and a process to handle those clients. Essentially, this meant I needed to create *a* business before I could call it mine.

In the first two years of my business, I had no process and no team. When it comes down to it, this meant that I had no business. The only thing I had to show for "my business" was a shell of a brand under which I operated. It had my name, my photo, and me as a worker.

Originally, my reasoning was that I operated on the premise of "supporting small business." I thought that by representing my work with pictures of me and my family, people would be more willing to show support.

It wasn't until later that I realized a business is meant to scale and to hold value for someone else to take over one day. Instead of limiting my business by keeping it to me and my family's "small" brand, I should have built with the intention of creating a successful operation that could go on without me.

This misguided attempt at a business was at the root of my work-to-survive cycle –it enslaved me to being the sole owner, operator, and employee. The first step to breaking free from my work-to-survive cycle meant creating a team that would help me and eventually take over for me. They would be able to help design events during the week and deliver the events on the weekend. As a result, I would be free to do higher-level work that continued to bring in money and clients.

In order to do this, though, I needed a process. I needed a flow created by set standards and procedures that my team would follow, creating consistency for the quality of work. Whether I was involved or not, all of my events could be fulfilled in accordance with my standard of excellence.

In the development of my business team, I brought on independent contractors because I realized it would help me to fine-tune my leadership skills, develop a process, and streamline my business growth.

In evaluating my need for independent contractors as opposed to employees from a legal perspective, I understood that the hours I had available for hire were more project-based rather than consistent. Instead of maintaining a team of employees who wouldn't have a steady flow of work to perform, I could hire contractors on an as-needed basis. I also understood that with independent contractors, I wasn't obligated to provide health insurance benefits or create a certain legal structure that I otherwise would be required to by law for employees. At the current size of my business, keeping my legal structure the same and avoiding offering benefits made more sense.

From a growth perspective, I realized that independent contractors were specialists in particular skill sets and had a need to grow their own business by providing quality work. Because of this motivation, I felt that I could trust them to always show up to every job offering me their full potential. In addition, I could treat these jobs like having a long-term working interview to evaluate their work style before deciding to offer a part-time or full-time position in the future.

WELCOME TO THE ROOM, MAMA

As a leader, I was able to fine-tune my process and iron out the kinks of having new people work in my business other than myself. I learned to delegate tasks, systemize the way that I operate so that it can be duplicated by my staff, and improve my organization and communication skills so that my team could perform to my business's best quality of service.

To ensure that the team members had everything they needed to fulfill each event, I needed to fine-tune my own procedures and create a manual of sorts. I needed a consistent approach to filing all the client information and everything discussed during our meetings. In doing this, I would always be on the same page with my clients and my team.

Streamlining my entire business's process from lead conversion to fulfillment of the contract was my top priority. The less time I needed to spend manually doing every task, the more time I could spend growing the business. Efficiency and perfection were at the core of everything.

Improving the efficiency of my business flow taught me that using the right tools and resources were key to my success for organized communication and planning.

I invested in software that would help make my notes easy to read and distribute to team members. It would give them all of the information they needed to complete the event.

In addition, I invested in different client relationship management systems that automatically scheduled content to be sent out at the right times, ensuring both my team and my clients had all of the information when they needed it.

Aside from digital organization, I also invested in organizational systems for our design studio so that our team members could find everything without needing us to be present.

- -

Repeat after me: A business is not a business if it cannot operate without your intervention. So, by automating as much as possible and building the process for the team, your business will have assets, procedures, and a continuous flow of leads and successful sales so that it can be an asset rather than a time and energy drain for your family.

In every step of your process building, keep in mind that you need flow. There needs to be an ease of operation at every step of your business's process. This free flow will better inspire creativity, increase efficiency, and boost morale within your work environment.

The most important aspect of breaking free from the work-to-survive cycle process involves creating a playbook of systems that take the business from "me-centered" to "team-centered."

A business that easily operates without you will actually build up trust with your clients. They'll see your business as reliable and stable, well-established and ready for anything. You'll be able to focus more on the personal human touches they need, like communicating their fears with them so that they feel at ease. Even your team will feel and work better because they'll have the tools, communication, and materials they need to fulfill their duties without your interference.

Limiting Mindset #16: "They'll never take me seriously enough to pay me what I want."

I have had approximately three leads in the last three months for wedding clients. We would hop on the phone for about forty-five minutes, and I'd send them the proposal soon after. Then, crickets. That silence sometimes feels worse than the sound of someone else's shit clunking at the bottom of the toilet in my old office job.

At the time, I let that silence get to me. I couldn't understand what went wrong or what I could do to finally convert those leads into real weddings I could serve. Was it that I didn't seem serious, official, professional, or experienced? Were my prices too high? Maybe they didn't want to work with someone who would have kids screaming in the background of every phone call, or who didn't have a physical storefront to visit.

My bedroom, after all, was my office. Anyone who works from home will tell you that it's not as fun as it sounds. When you're trying to be taken seriously while selling a wedding for five thousand dollars, having a baby climbing all over you and screaming isn't exactly any help.

Phone calls and babies don't mix well. It definitely doesn't say, "I'm the professional." The worst part is that I felt like I couldn't escape that reality, either.

One particular day, my phone buzzed with a familiar name. Her son was getting married in three weeks, and they were desperate for some flowers.

The text read, "Are you available?" I thought, *are you kidding?!* I replied, "I'll be over tonight to discuss the event."

One thousand dollars. A whopping one thousand dollars to bring a wedding to life with my flowers. A check that paid in full. Ecstatic at the prospect of finally making some money, I placed my order that night with my wholesaler.

In my rush, I only had pen and paper with me and a rough contract. That measely document definitely wouldn't have held up in court, but it would suffice for my needs today. *Nothing was going to go wrong, anyway*, I thought, *these are old friends of the family*. I was certain they'd spread word around town about my business, and I'd have beautiful professional photos from the event to finally show off to potential clients. My business was surely growing.

When the day came, I packed up my order. I told the bride I'd bring some extra flowers for the cake as my own little gift. I walked in with the biggest smile on my face, my baby belly knocking against the box of flowers I held in front of me. As I showed her the order, her face drops. She counts through all of the items.

"There's only seven bridesmaid bouquets here. We have eight bridesmaids. Boutonnieres, too, for the groomsmen."

I internally screamed. *What?* I quickly showed her exactly what they ordered, that I only fulfilled what was asked of me.

"Oh, can you make another one really quick?"

Thankfully, I had brought my tools with me. I decided to use the extra florals that I had originally brought for the cake. I was missing a few items to make them as full as the other bridesmaids, of course, but I managed to make them compliment the other bouquets. Proud of my savvy innovative thinking, I was sure they'd be so happy I was able to pull this one off for them.

With a renewed smile on my face, and a signed confirmation that they understood I'd invoice them later for the extra items, I drove off. When I returned home, I sent the extra invoice for the additional bouquet & boutonniere and privately celebrated my first official wedding.

Until… I got the phone call. I had just stepped out of the shower, feeling refreshed and excited for the big business I was creating. I was repeating affirmations to myself, "I am a wedding florist now, and nothing can hold me back."

I picked up the phone, expecting a thank you from my most recent client. Instead, I got: "Is this Alyssa? Hi, we received your invoice. I don't understand why you're charging us for an additional bouquet and boutonniere. It only took you ten minutes to make them."

Was I hearing this correctly? If you went to a restaurant and asked the chef to make an additional two meals instead of the seven meals that you originally ordered, would he not charge you for the two additional meals?

I tried to remain calm and reason with her. "Yes, I made two additional items. They were not in your original order, so you were not yet charged for them. When I was asked to create two more items to account for the additional bridesmaid and groomsmen, your husband signed off on the charges."

What I didn't express out loud was my guilt. Frustration. Anger. Fear. Anxiety. Resentment.

Even now, the pangs of frustration and anger hit me when I think of this conversation. I made a critical error: I let the client know how much time I spent creating their items. Even though any business owner will tell you that time is not the only reason to charge money, clients often see only that aspect of your work. That false sense of "ease," without consideration for the inconvenience, my expertise, what I paid for the items, let alone the ridiculous turnaround required, caused my client to believe my work was worth zero dollars.

Not just that it was worth nothing, but that they now threatened to never refer my business to anyone.

I took a hard step back and reevaluated my decisions. Is this still something I want to do? How can I learn from this to make sure it never happens again?

I considered the ways successful businesses operate. I thought back to how it was when I planned my own wedding. I took a deep dive into the needs that my clients have, which I now realize go much deeper than receiving the flowers.

At the end of the day, they need to feel like they made a good decision when hiring you. They need to feel excited for their upcoming day without stressing about their vendors. They need to feel like they're your only client, even though it's obvious that they're not.

How can I create this experience so that I'll be protected and they'll feel secure in their relationship with me? I need a process. I need to create a standard of operations, policies that I follow across the board, no matter the client. I need to look and feel official, professional, and polished –like I've done one hundred weddings in just this past year. They need to feel that, in the midst of pure wedding planning chaos, I'm the rock they can hold onto.

Integrity. Honesty. Communication. Professionalism. Experience.

These are the pillars that I now run my business on.

Through trial and error, I have built a robust and polished process that my clients can easily navigate. Many nights, I spent hours testing new email sequences, comparing my booking rate against different sales procedures and processes, updating my website, creating process documents, trialing packages, and experimenting with different variations of the industry standard pricing gauge.

As a professional, I set the standard for the way that my business operates. I take charge and remain an authority figure, walking them through every step of the process. I walk my prospective clients through what they can expect from their beautiful day, explaining everything about their wedding experience from their decor specifics to the timeline.

I am their guide. I help them envision exactly how their memories will be created. I show how my role in their wedding helps solve many of their problems, and I help them feel at ease throughout their planning. By giving clients the experience of a well-oiled process, I position myself as the expert for their event.

They feel at ease in the process, knowing what to expect and when. This beautifully laid out and reliable process is what differentiates me from the competition in my area –most local small businesses don't conduct themselves in such a neat and tidy way. It turns my home office into a city corner office. It turns my screaming children into classy personal assistants. It turns my young small-town floral design business into an industry institution.

And I will deliver items for their wedding day that are far better than they can imagine.

My clients will never "not refer my business to anyone" ever again.

- -

The client experience is at the heart of your business. Without taking a look at how your business will be experienced by an outsider, you won't be able to analyze it objectively or find flaws in your process. By showing that you care about the client experience, you'll build trust. You'll build great relationships with your clients, and that is a differentiator between you and your industry peers.

When creating your client experience, you have complete control over how your business looks from the outside. You can create this process to be as true-to-you as you want it to be. In other words, you can design your process to play to your strengths. For example, if you are a pro in face-to-face conversation, then you can design your process to incorporate Zoom meetings as an essential part of your sales process. Or, if you trip up in face-to-face presentations, phone conversations might be your best bet to close the deal. If you love sending gifts or cards, consider personalizing their experience with sweet gifts they receive as they work with you. The way the client experience is built will be unique for every business as they cater to the needs of their ideal clients and play to their strengths.

The best part of crafting this unique client experience is that it will become increasingly clear why your prospects should pick you over your peers. As leads enter your sales funnel, they can be sent a quick informal email and left to fend for themselves. OR they can be lead through a luxury experience where a deep connection is made through a comprehensive inquiry form, face-to-face discovery meeting, and continuous support throughout their decision-making process.

Walk in a prospect's shoes as you evaluate your business. How do they take the first step to engage with you, and what made them finally pull the trigger? What was your first interaction with them, and how did they respond to this communication? Do you ever follow-up after a period of silence from them, and do you send them any resources that help sway them towards hiring you?

During the inquiry process, take the opportunity to set the expectations for what it's like to do business with you. Of course, once they've hired you, make sure you deliver on those expectations. Your follow-through makes them excited to work with you even more and can result in raving reviews later.

Creating a process and communicating it well helps you to appear as a professional –and better yet, book the client. The more you follow through on your process, improve it, and communicate it with your prospects, the more professional you will look compared to your peers in the industry.

Phase 4: Nothing Changes If Nothing Changes, Mama. Make the Change.

As a mom-preneur, we will be faced with the need to take action, even when our mindset makes it feel like we're going to fail. We will have to be decisive, even when our mindset makes us feel guilty for taking action. We will have to push through when we're so exhausted that we feel like we can't take another step.

With the right plan in place to begin your entrepreneurial journey, your most important step will be the first one you take, no matter the step. No matter how big or how small. This first step will create the momentum needed to create the business we've planned together.

With each step you take, you'll be faced with new challenges as you grow and develop in your new roles. You'll face scarcity mindsets that make you hesitate when investing in your business. You'll have to rewrite the book for how you use your money. You'll need to grow into a leader with the confidence and organization to set your team and clients at ease.

Throughout this chapter, you'll take the final steps with me as I tell you about my own mindset barriers surrounding running and growing my business. I'm proud to say I've overcome them on my journey, but they still sit in the back of my mind. It's very likely you'll experience the same mindset barriers, so I want you to take heart in my experiences and apply my lessons learned as you begin to take action in your business.

In your workbook, I recommend that you follow along and complete the action items that correspond with each mindset barrier. Let's make the change, mama.

WELCOME TO THE ROOM, MAMA

Limiting Mindset #17: "I don't understand how to finance my business, so I'm too scared to spend my money." "

I felt like a failure. The success of my business weighed heavily on my ability to be self-disciplined, intelligent, and savvy with my client's money so that I could fulfill the event we envisioned together. Instead, I was struggling to keep the appropriate balance required in my checking account to even pay for my cost of goods sold.

How did it get like that? I told myself it's because I had just started my business, and that it's not uncommon for businesses to go without profit for the first two to five years of work.

But I knew that I was receiving payment in advance for services not yet rendered. I should simply just put the money aside diligently so that I would have it later to pay my expenses. I would have the money to pay my staff, purchase hardgoods and supplies, and to bring the whole vision to life.

Self-discipline with money is difficult for anyone. If you don't build the skillset of financial hygiene, whether it's for your personal bank accounts or for business, it's very difficult to ever see profit. For me, it was even more difficult to learn this lesson and apply good financial habits when I was not yet established in any way, shape, or form. This would be a new level of money mastery and I would be starting at the lowest level.

My old positions never required financial discipline, and I never previously considered financial discipline a weakness of mine.

In the past, I had worked tirelessly to successfully pay off fifteen thousand dollars of credit card debt in just eight months' time. Of course, with twenty-twenty hindsight vision, I realized that I lacked the discipline to prevent that debt from accruing in the first place.

There I was, personal debt on the rise again. I was motivated to finally flex the financial discipline muscle as I stood unwavering in my promises to fulfill my contracts.

Big lesson learned: I needed to know myself, strengths and weakenesses, in order to successfully run my business. By knowing where I fell short, I could strategically hire a team of people with strengths I didn't have. They would be able to help make up for my weaknesses in my business –especially when it came to getting my bookkeeping under control.

This issue was especially true in the early days of financial discipline when developing Garden In The Pines. It didn't help that every transaction I attempted to reconcile in my books had triplicated in my system, making everything messier by the day.

QuickBooks was not a skill I had been gifted with at an early age, so I quickly realized I could not fix these triplicated transactions. Don't chalk it up to lack of trying, because I dedicated more time than I ever should have to learning all of the functionalities and tools.

When my busiest event season came up on my calendar, I glanced at my accounts. With very little money, I realized I was doing a disservice to my business, my family, and my future clients. I needed to stop the bleeding at the wound itself so my business could fully heal.

Ironically, my time spent trying to rectify these issues ended up being even more of a waste of money and energy. Tax season was quickly approaching, and I would actually be smarter with my money if I hired a competent bookkeeper.

I am not a bookkeeper. I have no desire to be a bookkeeper. I would never make money being a bookkeeper. So why was I wasting a second of my time trying to get my books organized myself? Why wouldn't I hire a professional to do it faster and better than me?

Picking up the phone to admit I needed help, that was hard to swallow. To hire someone to help me in this task was to admit that I don't know it all. That I have weaknesses.

What pushed me through was realizing that it actually makes me a stronger business owner to admit my flaws and actively seek team members whose strengths are my weaknesses.

Admitting I needed help was going to be the saving grace of my business, and it would improve any future business I took on, too. That simple act of humility would change my family's future forever.

After all was said and done, I knew I had made the right decision. It took my professional team of bookkeepers six months to get my books in order. Let me say that again. It took six months of time with their combined professional skill sets, years of practice, and dozens of tools and programs.

Imagine if I had continued to stumble along trying to fix this myself? I would be doing a disservice to my business by trying to perfect a skill I had no interest pursuing for the sake of saving $600 a month, especially when it involved the financial health and wellness of my business.

Finally, my scarcity mindset was blown away. Money is a tool. Money can be used to create more time, which is more time you can spend making more money. It means less time and frustration working on my books, and more time creatively growing my business, developing marketing strategies, and creating financial freedom for my family.

And, with my bookkeepers implementing the profit-first method that I needed so desperately in my business, I finally had money to bring home to my family and to allocate for future business.

- -

You always hear the saying, "It takes money to make money." While this is true, if you don't have enough to money to dump into the business, it can really hinder your business growth. More importantly, though, if you don't use the money you have *wisely*, it won't matter if you start off with enough money. Soon, it'll be gone and you'll have nothing to show for it.

Think about it: you need money to hire a team, pay for software, fund the tools and physical workspace. You need money for marketing, or ads, or tickets. You need money for courses, workshops, and networking events. You need money for manufacturing, packaging, and shipping.

Every single aspect of your business needs money. It is the bloodline for the business. It keeps it pumping and moving, and if it ever runs out, there is nothing you can do to keep moving forward. If you started off with a few thousand dollars in starter money, but you blew it all on a bad investment instead of putting it where it mattered, you're done.

In the case that you don't have starter money yet, you could take loans. Loans can fuel the growth of your business quickly so that you can start seeing some of your own money. Some entrepreneurs decide to self-fund the business without loans or investors, but their growth is often much slower.

No matter how you get the money, you need the money. Without money, it makes it very difficult to hire or purchase the team, tools, or equipment you need to keep doing business. That means that you also can't hoard the money because you're scared of using it. The money is meant to be used to fuel your growth.

As a business owner, it's critical to take on as much money as you can early on. It will help you hire the right people to bring the vision to life and keep moving forward according to your marketing strategy, analytics, and successes. Or, like in my case, it will help you hire an accountant or bookkeeper so you can use your money for growth. Getting as much momentum as possible as soon as possible will mean profitability.

To do this right, financial management and budgeting should be a top priority when operating your business. You need to understand your numbers, how to properly delegate funds for marketing and operating expenses, and to learn how to analyze your results.

Budgeting with success in mind requires your ability to reflect on your income, expenses, and percentage allocations each week. You'll need to ensure you're not over-spending or under-spending. I want to emphasize that if you're underspending in certain areas, that could be contributing to a lack of growth.

As an example, here is how I have learned to allocate my finances for my business. This percentage breakdown ensures that all of my needs are met to run my business, but it also creates funds that I can use to fuel growth. I advise you to work with your accountant to discuss how this could look for your business as well.

Out of 100% of revenue coming into my business, I will allocate funds based on the following percentages:

- 20% of my revenue will be allocated for cost of goods sold (CGS)
- 15% of my revenue will be allocated for taxes
- 6.625% of my revenue will be allocated for sales tax
- 58% of my revenue will be allocated for business growth

Depositing your CGS-allocated funds immediately into a separate account always ensures that your clients get what they need. You should never feel like you have to borrow from Peter to pay John.

Allocating funds to save for your taxes will help to eliminate surprises at the end of the year. No more frantically scrounging up any last minute revenue possibilities because you can't afford your tax bill. Working with your accountant for tax planning will help you to understand your books and what you can afford to allocate to different areas of your business. They can also find specific tax deductions and benefits for your business to lower what you owe for the year and strategize for the years to come.

Likewise, distributing sales tax immediately into a separate account will help you to always have the funds to pay your sales tax bills. Eliminate your stress by taking this allocation directly off the top.

I break down that 58% allocated to business growth into more sections:

- 5% allocation to emergency fund
- 10-15% allocation to self-development and business coaching
- 25-35% allocation to team expenses & salaries
- 20% allocation to marketing
- 25-40% allocation to owner pay

Your emergency fund will be for those "just-in-case" scenarios or future opportunities that you don't want to miss out on. For example, perhaps a supplier that you use regularly is having a one-day sale, and taking advantage of it now would save you a large amount of money. Your emergency fund will come in handy to invest in that opportunity. Of course, the more traditional scenario would be to use that fund for an emergency situation like a leak in your building, faulty equipment, or higher-than-expected taxes.

As we've discussed in past chapters, development of yourself personally and professionally is crucial to your business success. Because of that reality, I recommend allocating funds directly into a budget for "self-development and business coaching."

When it comes to investing in your team, it's a must. Your team is an asset, and as we've discussed, you will always be the business if you don't have a team to run the business without you. Allocating funds for this budget will ensure that you're able to grow as a true stand-alone business.

You'll also need to prioritize reaching out to leads, because without leads, you'll never have a chance at capital. Your marketing budget is the source of acquiring a larger audience.
The exciting thing about using percentages for allocation is that the amount of funds will keep growing exponentially. Exponentially growing funds means an exponentially growing business.

As an entrepreneur and small business owner, the hardest lesson to learn is that your business revenue is not a personal paycheck. You should never immediately deposit all your profit into your personal account and call it a day because so much of that money has already been dedicated to running your business. Of course, you'll want to take some money home, so allocating your funds based on the above percentages will help you to fuel your business growth while also maintaining a decent pay.

Taking this profit-first approach directly from the incoming revenue will ensure that you're always paid, but your business will still have the money it needs to live on.

Of course, depending on your type of business, you may need to adjust these percentages accordingly.

To identify these numbers for yourself, you'll need to consider your situation, goals, and personal needs. If you haven't already done so, it's most important to create a budget based on your income and expenses. Remind yourself of your goals upfront so you can decide what is important in your life at this time.

As a young mom-preneur, perhaps your goals are to simply support your family with your new business. You might not be planning world domination —at least, not yet. You know your personal expenses, needs, and your goals more than I do. In this case, perhaps your value at the moment is generating a higher salary from your business, even if that means prolonging your journey of business growth.

Rest assured, these allocation percentages are controlled by *you*. At any time, should your needs and priorities change, you can immediately alter the percentages.

Ask these questions in your local business communities, in your mom-preneur groups, or over in our Facebook group "Making Mommy Moves with Lyss Morton" You can find the link in our resource section. Creating a conversation around this topic can help unveil unique ways of budgeting for your personal needs and business growth. Use the room that you've created to your advantage so that you can continually work toward accomplishing your goals.

Limiting Mindset #18: "I could never do sales."

The wedding inquiries continued to come, and my branding was up to par now, but I still felt like I was struggling to communicate with my prospects to close sales.

I need to learn sales.

An invitation to join a sales mastermind group popped up in my inbox as I rocked my newborn to sleep for the third time that night. It started in just a couple days and consisted of a group of luxury wedding professionals. *Invest now so you can continue to grow your business on the right foot,* I say to myself, yet again. A rush of exhilaration, or probably fear, came over me as I invested another six thousand dollars into myself and my business growth.

Investing nearly fifteen thousand dollars in the course of a month is a lot when you've got two kids under two. Especially when you don't even have that much currently in your checking account. Though, with an easy-to-navigate website decked out in gorgeous branding and my new sales skills, this investment was sure to pay dividends forever.

In learning from experts, I realized that my sales strategy was non-existent. Worse yet, my sales mindset was non-existent. Before the course, I would attempt to get the prospect on the phone and adjust the price to meet their budget, even if it resulted in a different wedding than they had envisioned. Can you believe that was the best case scenario? Other times, I would drop the price and still deliver what they wanted, even though I was the one paying for it.

All of these terrible decisions originated from one ugly mindset: I felt that I wouldn't spend the money on my own service, so why would someone else?

In the mastermind group, I learned the importance of building value in the conversation. To get prospects to convert, you needed to convince them that your value as a business went beyond just offering the service they needed. You had to show them that you have the perfect business to do the job.

Part of building value in the sales conversation is first understanding the priorities of your prospects. You need to genuinely understand what they see as valuable before you can show that value to them. In the group, we discussed that there are different people in different status groups, and these backgrounds cause them to value different things.

For example, budget brides value saving as much money as possible on their wedding. This value might naturally come from not being able to afford more expensive vendors, or from a struggle with a financial scarcity mindset of their own. Overall, they don't value spending a large amount of money on the wedding experience because a house, trip, or other financial responsibilities are more important to them. In turn, the budget bride would not be the ideal audience for a business that offers luxury floral designs. A luxury floral design business would not likely be able to convert these prospects because they cannot offer the value that a budget bride desires.

On the other hand, upper-middle class and upper-class individuals might enjoy the rush of organizing and hosting larger, more extravagant events. They might value the beauty that floral design creates in a space, and they could enjoy seeing their guests' faces light up when the environment is transformed by the use of floral design at their event. Thus, they value spending whatever it takes to have this experience for their guests.

As I started showing up to the bi-weekly meetings, I started to think about the many floral designers in my surrounding community. Most of the local florists I knew struggled with their mindsets. They couldn't get themselves to charge clients appropriately for the services that they were providing. They kept trying to be everything to everyone, just to stay afloat.

When I think about it now, it's seriously a wonder how they're able to keep the lights on in the studio. I don't know how they keep paying staff to help design, or can afford to pay for the flowers for their events. I can't imagine that they take a salary.

The costs of flowers keeps rising since the pandemic, yet no one's prices seem to be adjusting. Most florists would keep with the status quo for fear of losing out to competition. This course made me realize that if I couldn't keep the lights on, there was no point in trying to stay in business.

As my mindset evolved, so did my prices and the way that I spoke to clients. Suddenly, I was able to communicate value because I knew my value, and I believed in it.

Overall, I took advantage of the experts who had the skills that I didn't. I learned to reframe my money mindsets, ditched my imposter syndrome, and re-affirmed that I had every right to follow my passion as a floral designer. It didn't matter if this was only my first year of event floral design, or my first try ever at building a business. With better attitudes about my worth, my business's value, and my money, I could attract the best clients for my business and stop comparing myself to everyone else.

- -

When you focus on sales-related limiting beliefs, your prospective clients can feel your uncertain energy.

Your prospective clients need to feel understood. They need to feel that you can solve their problem and do it with reliability. They need to be convinced that any amount is worth investing to solve their problem and create the experience they want.

To overcome your own limiting beliefs as an entrepreneur and boost sales in your business, we need to outline all of your limiting beliefs surrounding sales and money.

Dump it all on paper. The act of physically writing this out on paper is freeing for your mind. It helps you to step out of yourself momentarily to look at the big picture.

What are your limiting mindsets? Do they look something like mine did?

"Selling is slimy."

"People don't like to be solicited."

"I will never be financially successful."

"Money doesn't grow on trees."

"I wouldn't spend money on that."

When you spell out all of your limiting mindsets on paper, you'll be able to take the first step in shifting those mindsets. You'll be able to replace those mindsets with your new-found belief in your worth. Anytime you feel those mindsets creep back into your mind again, repeating your new beliefs will help you to feel empowered in your sales conversations.

Some mindsets you can use to replace those old beliefs are:

"Selling is serving."

"People will pay anything to solve a problem they are experiencing."

"I am financially successful."

"Money is abundant, and it is flowing to my business."

"My clients value my service enough to pay any price tag."

Remove those feelings of scarcity from your body and mind, and suddenly you will open up to receive more abundance.

Limiting Mindset #19: "I can't step away from my business because no one will run my business like me."

I missed every single weekend this summer with my kids. I missed almost every single family dinner. I missed too many baths, too many stories, and too many hugs before bed.

I missed my baby's first birthday. And my baby's second birthday.

Time slips away ever so quickly as I work tirelessly to make this happen for my family.

I had prioritized my business baby, and now I was fighting to gain back the missed time with my real babies.

You and I both know that we can't gain any time back, but I could maximize the time that remained to make the rest of their childhood fun. I could do my best to create memories they'll cherish forever, and ensure the financial security to do the things that bring them joy.

Sometimes, ego can make you blind. I felt blind to all of the solutions around me because I needed to figure this business out on my own.

My ego was so large that I felt like I needed to be the person to do everything in my business. Except I could not, and I should not. Instead, it cost me time that could have been spent with my children.

How stupid could I have been? Why tire myself out each night, potentially delivering subpar work, because I needed to be the person to create it?

Once I realized this huge mistake, I hired help in my business.

The first time that I hired a freelancer, it was a triple-header event weekend. Quite simply, I just had no choice but to get extra hands if I was going to deliver on my contracts. What I anticipated would be the most stressful weekend ended up being the best weekend I had ever experienced as a business owner. I was able to fulfill three events with the help of this freelance staff member, all because she headed up design in my studio for the other events so that I could make the deliveries and set up for each event.

It truly felt like I was able to be in two places at the same time.

In preparation for the additional help, I organized all of the tools so that they would be easily accessible. I created documents with the notes about the florals for each event, how the arrangements should look, and all the other details she would need to fulfill the events. All just as I would have done it myself.

I had trusted her wealth of experience in the industry. She understood the vision. Because I had done work to build my leadership skills, I was able to let go of full control and let her design with my guidance. Any problems that arose, I knew we could solve together without undue stress because she was giving me more time.

- -

We've touched on this a bit already, but businesses that rely on the owner to physically show up daily and do the work are simply just another job that drains the employee. An entrepreneur that is shackled to their business will never be able to scale and grow to their full potential. That business will always be dependent on the entrepreneur to fulfill the work.

That business will never allow for family dinners, bedtime routines, or extra hugs.

Businesses that are built on the promise of "I will be there," instead of "my team has the know-how, talent, and guidance to follow through on your success," will never create financial security. More importantly, this kind of business is built on ego rather than leadership.

The concept of business ownership needs to be flipped on its head for your greater good. You might think you need to be the be-all-end-all of your business, but you'll soon realize that's unsustainable, and it really doesn't serve the purpose of why you became an entrepreneur in the first place.

Time needs to be the currency that we work to be paid. We need to be working to create more time in our life. Money is only the tool to create more time. Use money to delegate more tasks and create more speed. Money doesn't have to be evil, or conniving, or a vice. It doesn't have to be a problem or a catastrophe waiting to happen.

If any amount of time spent performing a task takes you away from scaling your business or enjoying your babies, then you should be fighting to get that time back as much as possible.

Leadership is a critical skill needed for business growth. As business leaders, we need to empower our team to make important decisions, learn from their mistakes, and grow in their positions.

Leadership requires us to remove the ego from our business. It means we have to believe that others are better than us at certain things, and that our weaknesses could be countered by their strengths, giving us a solid business across the board.

When an issue arises in the business, we need to address our own leadership skills rather than pass on the blame to others. We need to discover what we can do better next time to encourage solutions, prevent mistakes from happening, and create processes that allow for seamless business operations. We must create an environment for free creativity and flow within our organization.

Leaders don't micromanage staff members, hover over their shoulders, and seek constant reassurance. Leaders inspire their team. They create a judgment-free and backlash-free space for ideas. They allow for creative solutions, even if it's not the way that they would do things, because they know that they hired an expert for the position. Ultimately, they fully believe in their team's capabilities, so they give them the support and freedom to thrive

When issues arise in your business, question your leadership.

Developing your leadership skills will enable you to run a full and successful team, leaving more time on your plate to spend doing the things that bring you joy. You'll be able to focus on your passions, create your community, and soak in every second with your family before it's too late.

An added benefit that I enjoy is that it will also help you create the opportunities for others that you once needed –to work with other professionals so that you could gain experience to start your own business. Once you've become a leader and a successful business owner, it's time for you to step aside and create that space for others.

Becoming A Mompreneur

Self-development is at the core of entrepreneurship as well as being a mother. My hope is that this book has given you a leg-up so that you feel empowered and prepared to take on anything. The mindsets that present themselves repeatedly throughout your journey might have crushed you before, but now, you can see them as opportunities to completely turn your life around and achieve your vision.

Inevitable changes occur to everyone that suddenly finds themselves in charge of other human beings —both babies and staff. It's common to be overwhelmed by all your passions and drives, especially when they seem to be at odds with each other. You'll have to make hard decisions about what to prioritize, and you'll need to master focusing on the big picture, the long game, and your reason why.

Feelings like a lack of direction, imposter syndrome, fear of failure, perfectionism, and a lack of support will often add to your loneliness and overwhelm. As you overcome your self-doubt, battle mom guilt, prioritize self-care, and rectify your mismanagement of time, you might even encounter new limiting mindsets that further prevent you from moving the needle on your journey of entrepreneurship and self-development. I have done my best to cover them all, but you now have the tools to tackle any new challenges that come your way.

With renewed passion, self-confidence, self-care, and time management mastery, you can feel confident in starting to plan the business you've envisioned for your family –the vision that keeps you moving forward, networking with your peers, and fine-tuning your business process. The vision that holds you accountable and keeps your head high every time you get new feedback from a "failure."

And with your plans for success in place, your new room full of a supportive community, and a team that will help propel you forward, your business and your dreams will begin to grow right before your eyes.

By implementing my strategies, mindset success tips, and hard-learned lessons, you'll be able to shave years off your own entrepreneurial journey of trial and error, helping you achieve success in your business that much faster.

As a mom-preneur, you have the strength, tenacity, and resources now to bring your vision to fruition.

I encourage you to take this time to reflect on your needs, your vision, and your desires to manifest the life that you are passionate about. I encourage you to think about the needs you are going to fulfill in your community, the problems you are going to solve, and to use that as your fire to start.

Starting your journey is going to be the most important and most difficult step you take. The next difficult step you're going to take is to persevere against all odds. Follow through on your actions, create consistent momentum, and keep moving the needle on your goals.

No one is going to do the work for you. Mama… Just start.

Here's What To Do Next

Whenever you're ready, here are four ways that I can help you on your journey as a mom-preneur:

1. Access All Of Your Free Bonuses

By reading this book and saying "yes" to investing in yourself, you have unlocked every bonus and resource in this book.

Visit www.lyssmorton.com/book to get all the resources mentioned in this book for free.

2. Work 1-on-1 with Me

If you found this book helpful and want help in starting your mom-preneur journey, I'd love to invite you to chat with me.

Visit www.lyssmorton.com/book to schedule a call with me to discuss your needs and build a success plan.

3. Hire Me To Speak

If you are looking for a high-energy mama of a motivational speaker for your conference, event, podcast, or mastermind, I'd love to bring it!

Email Lyss@LyssMorton.com with "SPEAKING" in the subject line.

4. Connect On Social Media

Let's keep the conversation going. You're part of my room now, mama. The journey doesn't end here. I'd love to connect with you on all social platforms and in our free Facebook community.

You can find me here:

- Instagram: @Lyss.Morton
- Facebook: @Lyss.Morton
- Facebook Group: Making Mommy Moves with Lyss Morton
- YouTube: Lyss Morton
- TikTok: Lyss.Morton
- LinkedIn: Alyssa Morton
- Listen to the podcast: The Making Mommy Moves Show

Resources

Please find all of the free resources mentioned in our book, as well as our free workbook here: www.lyssmorton.com/book.

The tools and resources discussed in the book are explained below along with any affiliate codes I may have. If you decide to purchase these resources, I may receive a small commission at no additional cost to you.

Dubsado:

In my business, Dubsado is my client relationship management system that helps to automate my client experience. It keeps track of all of the events I have booked for the year and it syncs with my calendar so no dates are missed. It collects payments, sends payment reminders, creates easy-to-update payment schedules and due-dates. It also sends out information that I need and my clients need to complete according to the trigger schedule I set.

They receive automated emails so they feel they are top of mind, and so that they can complete things I need in a timely manner, like timeline questionnaires and detail confirmations.

Here's an example of my workflow through Dubsado: My prospective clients submit a Dubsado inquiry form through my website. This triggers a canned email response. They receive a questionnaire in the canned email with the ability to schedule a quick chat. We chat on the phone. In our proposal meeting, if they decide they want to move forward with Garden In The Pines they will receive a contract and proposal through Dubsado. The client is able to sign the contract electronically and pay through Dubsado's invoice. They receive scheduled emails throughout their planning process. I can edit the emails as needed to best suit their personality and wedding. It goes out automatically, so this creates a "set it and forget it" process for my business.

For my "al a carte" sales, clients are directed through my website to a public Dubsado proposal where they can select the items and quantities they want, pick a style that speaks to their soul, and upload a handful of inspiration images. They're directed to our contract and payment portal. They receive automated emails and questionnaires leading up to their wedding. We send a final confirmation that they can approve. We deliver their event according to the design style chosen.

You can receive 20% off your first month or first year of Dubsado with this link: https://www.dubsado.com/?c=GITP

You can find my Dubsado course here to set up your own al-a-carte system with my done-for-you questionnaires, emails, and resources:https://gardeninthepines.com/join-simple-weddings

For additional information about our done-for-you service to set up our "al a carte" ordering system in your own Dubsado account, contact us at hello@gardeninthepines.com.

Google Calendar:

Google Calendar is my lifeline in my business. I am able to sync tasks to multiple calendars, add reminders and follow-ups, and build in time to work on my business at the beginning of the year so that we are always growing. Google Calendar syncs with Asana, too, so everyone is always reminded of deadlines.

In addition, scheduling time for yourself into your calendar in Google will ensure that you are getting the time in each day to fill your cup. Making this a standard practice in your day will also ensure that this is the standard by which you operate, not the exception.

Calendly:

When you have the pre-scheduled time in your calendar to fill up your cup, you'll be able to integrate your calendar with Calendly so that it automatically schedules appointments at times that do not interfere with your Google calendars. Sync all of your calendars for work, personal life, and you-time with your Calendly application so that you are able to fulfill your obligations for your business and yourself.

With this integration, you respect your boundaries that you've created regularly so that your standard practice is to fill your cup first. You'll have the grace to make an exception when needed for a very important reason, but it will be standard practice to fill your cup first and respect the boundaries you've created.

Loom:

Loom is one of my favorite tools to record video tutorials. It makes it simple for me to record my screen and my face at the same time so I can best explain a process, how to use a website, or how to use our business tools.

In creating my business process, I use Loom to create my video tutorials for staff to easily see how I create a bouquet style, how I update a recipe in my computer system, how I print out a report, etc.

This makes it simple for another team member to pick up where I or another team member left off, and so that moving forward in the growth of my business, it is simple to train additional members of the team, scale, and potentially sell my business in the future.

You can get Loom here with my affiliate link:
https://loom.grsm.io/xs1e0lkw5zju

Google Spreadsheet:

I currently have my master playbook organized in a Google Spreadsheet. I am easily able to link my videos, staff is able to search keywords with the "Control/Command F" buttons, and I have it structured in a way that makes it easy to search my table of contents.

Asana:

Asana is one of my favorite tools to keep me organized. It is a project management software designed to help you stay on task and on deadline. There are automations that can be created to help delegate tasks when it moves to a certain stage in your project pipeline. And reminders, checklists, calendar-views, and boards are there to help you visualize your project however you need to see it so you can begin getting quality work completed on your project.

I use Asana across all of my businesses to keep track of the events we have happening, so that my social media calendar is current, and that when I need to order supplies for particular projects, I know exactly what and when. You name it.

Trellis:

In my floral design business, it is important that I have a backend system to ensure that I am pricing my events accordingly. This may look like a different system for your business, but I wanted to demonstrate the importance of staying on top of your numbers. It is also great for staying on task with your clients so no one is missed.

I use Trellis to calculate my recipe totals to ensure that I am not over-ordering. I've worked with other florists that "create a recipe in their head" and it looks like a mess on their books. Most of the time, they ordered way more flowers than they needed, sending their event over budget and affecting their profit margin. Not to mention, flowers are a perishable product, so there really is no "I can hold onto this and use it later."

Using a tool like Trellis has allowed my business to be more profitable. I love saving go-to recipes for future event use and minimizing my time spent in the process.

Acknowledgments

Writing a book is everything people say it is, and hard doesn't even begin to describe it. None of this would have been possible without my husband, Larry Morton. He kept me motivated, helped ensure that I had my book time each night, and empowered me when I felt like I was going way off base. His love, support, and encouragement brought this book to life.

My sweet daughters reminded me of my purpose in sharing my entrepreneurial journey with the world. For them, I will always do hard things… even when it includes admitting the deepest faults about myself to the world.

To my old boss, thank you for giving me all of the fuel I needed to become an entrepreneur. Without the experience that I endured in my small, four-foot by eight-foot "office," I wouldn't have been encouraged to envision my own business and find my values. I wouldn't have dreamed of the team I wanted to empower, and I wouldn't have had the passion to develop the skills needed to create my own business(es). I am eternally grateful.

To my long-time friend and editor, Brenna Mallozzi, thank you for helping point me in the right direction and encouraging me to write this book. Your past experiences in publishing helped empower me to start building my audience and two other businesses as a result of bringing this book to life!

A very special thanks to my coach, Jake Kelfer. Without your guidance, I would be lost in a sea of confusion and inaction due to the overwhelming process of getting a book into the world as a self-published author. Thank you from the bottom of my heart for giving me the motivation and stern kick in the ass when needed, too.

I'd like to thank my assistant, Rochelle Rae, for absolutely everything she did to help me through this process. She gave me the space to be creative while she began doing the leg work on our marketing strategy. I appreciate your attention to detail and excitement throughout the entire process!

I'd like to thank my team for putting this book together and making it legit! Cheers to you: my editor Brenna Mallozzi, the design team at 100 Covers, and my formatter, Polgarus Studio.

Finally, I'd like to thank YOU, my mom-preneur readers. Thank you for choosing to invest your time, money, and energy into reading this book. I can't wait to see all that you accomplish in this world with your future business. And, I'd like to officially say... Welcome To The Room, Mama.

About The Author

Alyssa Morton is a serial entrepreneur, mama of two, motivational speaker, and coach to ambitious mamas, helping mom-preneurs at heart start and scale their businesses. She enjoys working one-on-one with women to help them overcome their limiting beliefs and create a strategy for success in their life and business through her four-phase process. Alyssa is regularly featured on podcasts, summits, and stages to help empower moms to create the life they want for themselves. Connect with Alyssa on social at @lyss.morton.

Made in the USA
Middletown, DE
14 February 2023

24033068R00080